A Documentary Theoretical Approach to Digital Electronics Logic Design Digital Communication Basic C and Matlab Programming for Graduate Electrical and Electronics Students

Abir Chakraborty

TANEESHA
PUBLISHERS

Book Title   : A Documentary Theoretical Approach to Digital Electronics Logic
                Design Digital Communication Basic C and Matlab Programming
                for Graduate Electrical and Electronics Students

Author   : Abir Chakraborty

Edition No.   : First

Published on : October, 2024

ISBN   : 9789348037947

MRP   : Rs. 490/-

Published by

TANEESHA PUBLISHERS

A Venture by -
PRACHI DIGITAL PUBLICATION

Regd. Add.: 254, Khuriyakhatta No. 10, Bindukhatta,
Lalkuan, Nainital - 262402, Uttarakhand, India
Website : www.taneeshapublishers.in
E-mail : taneeshapublishers@gmail.com
Phone : +91 8454 812712, +91 8057 812712

Printed by :
Manipal Technologies Limited, Bengaluru - 560001, Karnataka

ABOUT THE AUTHOR

The author was an research associate of University of Coimbra , Portugal, has published many research articles on image processing .He has completed his Master of Technology degree from Manipal Academy of Higher Education, Karnataka. The research area of the author is image processing control system machine learning and signal processing. The author has worked with several types Jpeg and Png type images and has done several operations on images.

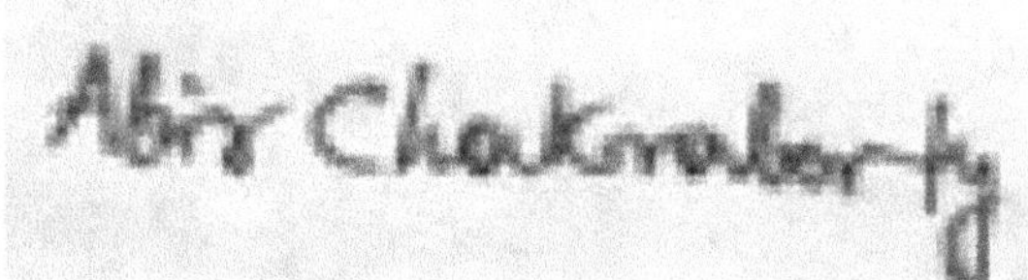

IDENTITY OF THE AUTHOR

FACEBOOK ID	abir Chakraborty.facebook
GOOGLE SCHOLAR ID	abir Chakraborty google scholar(Vellore institute of technology)
LINKEDIN ID	Abir-chakraborty-81689105 Abir-chakraborty-0a1043211
ACADEMIA.EDU ID	Abir Chakraborty.academia.edu
EMAIL ID	abir.cdauto@gmail.com

ACKNOWLEDGEMENT

Here author wants to show his full gratitude and honor to MANIPAL ACADEMY OF HIGHER EDUCATION, KARNATAKA and NATIONAL INSTITUTE OF TECHNOLOGY, ROURKELA (ODISHA) electronics and communication department from where author has collected the basic electronics related syllabus of electromagnetism and from these two engineering universities author has installed the latest version of matlab for his books and research articles publication purpose.

[ANNEXTURE BOOK-1]

DIGITAL ELECTRONICS THEORITICAL HANDBOOK OF GRADUATE ENGINEERING STUDENT

ABSTRACT

Digital electronics is a very important subject of electronics and communication engineering. This book is actually meant for graduate engineering students of electronics and communication and electrical engineering; because in these two departments digital electronics is a major subject. Actually it is a laboratory engineering handbook for graduate and diploma engineering students. But this book has a logical difference with digital electronics laboratory because in digital electronics laboratory because in digital electronics laboratory generally engineering colleges use digital logic trainer kit for laboratory experiment purpose; but in this book the author has used mat-lab software for programming purpose for each digital electronics laboratory experiments. That's why in order to understand the experiments author has first explained the theoretical part of several chapters before the commencement of programming. But all the chapters of experiments are related to graduation as well as diploma syllabus of electronics and electrical engineering only.

INDEX

SL NO	NAME OF THE CHAPTER	PAGE NO
1	INTRODUCTION	8
2	NUMBER SYSTEM IN DIGITAL ELECTRONICS	8-12
3	VERIFICATION OF TRUTH TABLE OF DIFFERENT LOGIC GATES AND BOOLEAN ALGEBRA	12-18
4	DIGITAL LOGIC CODE CONVERTER (Binary to gray code converter)	18-21
5	EXAMPLES OF ARITHMATIC LOGIC CIRCUIT a. HALF ADDER b. FULL ADDER c. HALF SUBSTRACTOR d. FULL SUBSTRACTOR	22-24
6	EXAMPLE OF COMBINATIONAL LOGIC CIRCUIT (MUX AND DECODER) a. HALF ADDER BY MULTIPLEXER b. FULL ADDER BY MULTIPLEXER c. DECODER CIRCUIT APPLICATION d. 2 BIT COMPARATOR	24-27
7	1'S COMPLEMENT AND 2'S COMPLEMENT	28-31
8	FLIP-FLOP CONSTRUCTION WITH WORKING PRINCIPLE AND TRUTH TABLE	31-39
9	FLIP FLOP CONVERSION	39-47
10	COUNTER AND REGISTER	48-50
11	LOGIC FAMILIES IN DIGITAL ELECTRONICS	48-50
12	CMOS VLSI GATE DESIGN LOGIC	50-51
13	PRGOAMMABLE LOGIC DEVICE	51-53
14	MEMORY DEVICE	53-56
15	A/D AND D/A CONVERTER	56-60
16	CONCLUSION	61

CHAPTER-1

INTRODUCTION

This book author is dedicating an electronics laboratory handbook for graduate and diploma electronics and electrical engineering students. Author is focusing only some basic digital electronics laboratory oriented basic and simple experiments. Practically author is focusing on the academic syllabus of diploma engineering students where number of laboratory related experiments are comparatively less. But only few important experiments author has mentioned in this book which can be used for diploma engineering handbook. Digital electronics related experiments can be done by using digital logic trainer kit. But here author has tried to use concept of very simple mat-lab coding to explain the digital electronics experiments. The aim of the author is to make the students aware about the latest and simple coding concept of mat-lab as per diploma and graduation level. So students are requested read and practice the mat-lab codes very carefully for which installation of mat-lab software is necessary in system.

CHAPTER-2

NUMBER SYSTEM IN DIGITAL ELECTRONICS

2.1 BOOLEAN ALGEBRA:

Theorem 1 (Operations with 0's and 1's)

    a. $0.x=0$
    b. $1+x=1$

Theorem 2 (Operation's with 0's and 1's)

    a. $1.x=x$
    b. $0+x=x$

Theorem 3 (Idempotent law or identity laws)

    a. $x.x.x.x.x.x\ldots\ldots\ldots x=x$
    b. $x+x+x+x+x+\ldots\ldots\ldots x=x$

Theorem 4 (complement law)

    a. $x.(x)'=0$

    b. $x+x'=1$

Theorem 5 (cumulative laws)

    a. $x+y=y+x$

    b. $x.y=y.x$

Theorem 6 (Associated law)

    a. $x+(y+z)=(x+y)+z=z+(x+y)$

Theorem 7 (Distributive laws)

    a. $x.(y+z)=x.y+y.z$

    b. $x+y.z=(x+y).(y+z)$

Theorem 8

    a. $x.y+x.y'=x$

    b. $(x+y).(x+y')=x$

Theorem 9

    a. $(x+y').x=x.y$

    b. $x.y'+y=x+y$

Applying distributive law

$(x.y'+y)=(x+y).(y+y')=x+y$

Applying complementation law

$y+y'=1$

$x.y+y=x+y$

Theorem 10 (Absorption law or redundancy law)

    a. $x+x.y=x$ $1+y=1$

    b. $x.(x+x')=x$

a. $x.y + y.z + x'.z = x.y + x'.z$

b. $(x+y)(x'+y).(y+z) = (x+y).(x'+z)$

2.2 Demorgan's theorem

It is an application to convert complementary or gate to complementary AND gate ,it is used to solve Boolean logic problem

a. $(x_1 + x_2 + x_3 + x_4 + x_5)' = x_1'.x_2'.x_3'.x_4'.x_5'$ b. $(x_1.x_2.x_3.x_4.x_5)' = x_1' + x_2' + x_3' + x_4' + x_5'$

2.3 What is number system in digital electronics

A number system is defined as a system of writing to express numbers. A number system is a mathematical system is a mathematical system base n , where n represents total numbers present in that system.

2.4 Digital code conversion

2.4.1 Binary to digital one example

$(111\ 0\ 111)_2 = (119)_{10}$

$\Rightarrow$ $1 \times 2^6 + 1 \times 2^5 + 1 \times 2^4 + 0 \times 2^3 + 1 \times 2^2 + 2 + 2^0 \times 1 = (119)_{10}$

2.4.2 Decimal to binary

$(120)_{10} = (1\ 1\ 1\ 1\ 0\ 0\ 0)_2$

2.4.3 Octal to binary

$(374.26)_8 = (011111100.010110)_2$

2.4.4 Binary to octal

001110100.010011100

001=1

110=6

100=4

010=2

011=3

100=4

(164.234)$_8$

2.4.5 Hexadecimal to Binary

(17E.F6)=(000101111110.11110110)$_2$

2.4.6 Binary to Hexadecimal

001011001110.011011101000

0010=2

1100=C

1110=E

0110=6

1110=E

1000=8

(2CE.6E8)$_{16}$

2.4.7 Hexadecimal to Octal

(2F.C4)$_{16}$ = (00101111.11000100)

101=5

111=7

110=6

001=1

(57.61)$_8$

2.4.8 Octal to Hexadecimal

(762.013)$_8$

7=111

6=110

2=010

0=000

1=001

3=011

0001=1

1111=F

0010=2

0000=0

0101=5

1000=8

=>$(1F2.058)_{16}$

CHAPTER-3

VERIFICATION OF TRUTH TABLE OF DIFFERENT LOGIC GATES AND BOOLEAN ALGEBRA

3.1 BASIC AND UNIVERSAL GATE DEFINITION:

The logic gates which are used to make fundamental Boolean circuits in digital electronics are called basic gates; example- AND, OR , NOT

The logic gates which are used to make all types of Boolean algebra circuits and every type of basic gates can be designed by using this gates in digital electronics are called universal gates; example- NAND, NOR.

3.2 *LOGIC GATES WITH CHIP NUMBER*

NAME OF THE GATES	IC CHIP NUMBER
AND	7408
OR	7432
NOT	7404
NAND	7400
NOR	7402
XNOR	74266

XOR	7486

3.3 SYMBOL OF LOGIC GATES WITH TRUTH TABLE

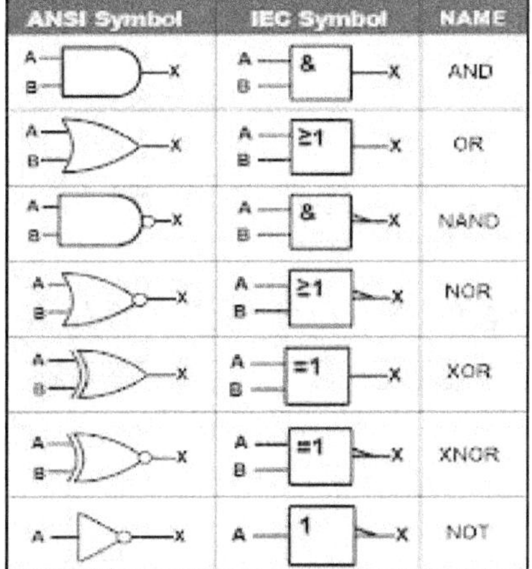

3.4 TRUTH TABLE OF ALL LOGIC GATES

NAME OF THE GATE	INPUT A	INPUT B	OUTPUT
AND	0	0	0
	0	1	0
	1	0	0
	1	1	1
OR	0	0	0
	0	1	1
	1	0	1
	1	1	1
NAND	0	0	1
	0	1	1
	1	0	1
	1	1	0
NOR	0	0	1
	0	1	0
	1	0	0
	1	1	0
XOR	0	0	0
	0	1	1

	1	0	1
	1	1	0
XNOR	0	0	1
	0	1	0
	1	0	0
	1	1	1
NOT	0		1
	1		0

3.5 *BOOLEAN FORMULAES OF ALL TWO INPUT LOGIC GATES*

NAME OF THE LOGIC GATE	BOOLEAN EXPRESSIONS
AND	$A*B$
OR	$A+B$
NOT	$A^/$
NAND	$(A*B)^/$
NOR	$(A+B)^/$
XOR	$A^/*B+A*B^/$
XNOR	$A*B+A/*B/$

3.6 *CONSTRUCTION OF BASIC GATES BY USING UNIVERSAL GATE:*

3.6.1 *AND GATE USING NOR GATE*

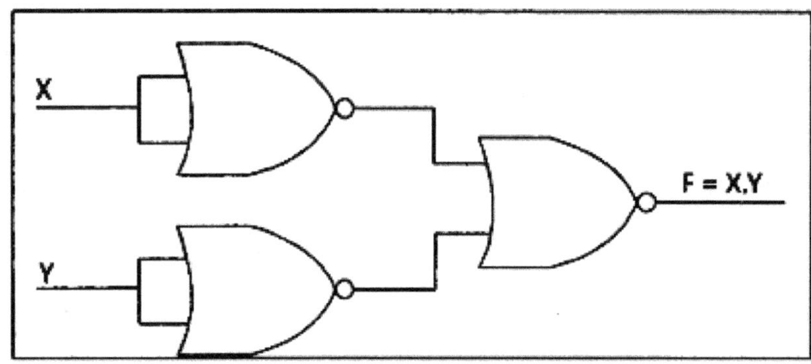

$F=(X^/+Y^/)^/=X*Y$

3.6.2 *OR GATE USING NOR GATE*

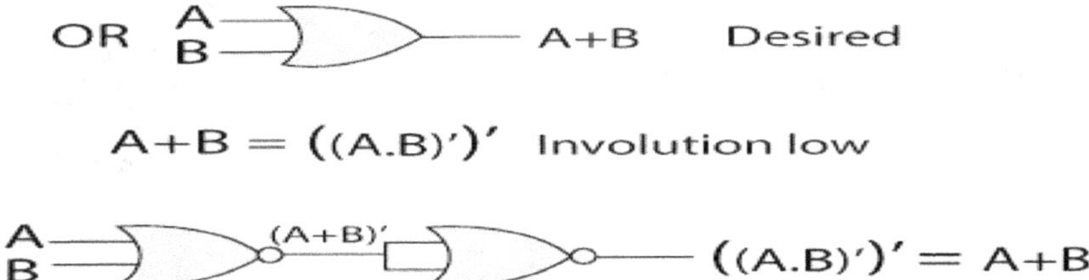

3.6.3 *NOT GATE USING NOR GATE*

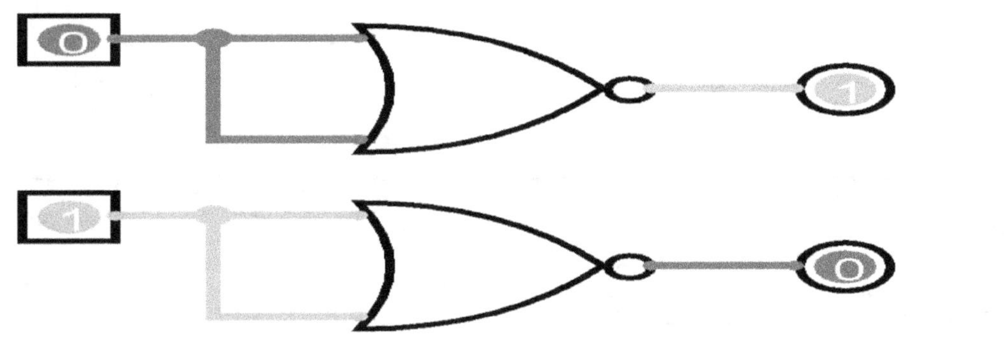

$$X=(A)'$$

3.6.4 *AND GATE USING NAND GATE*

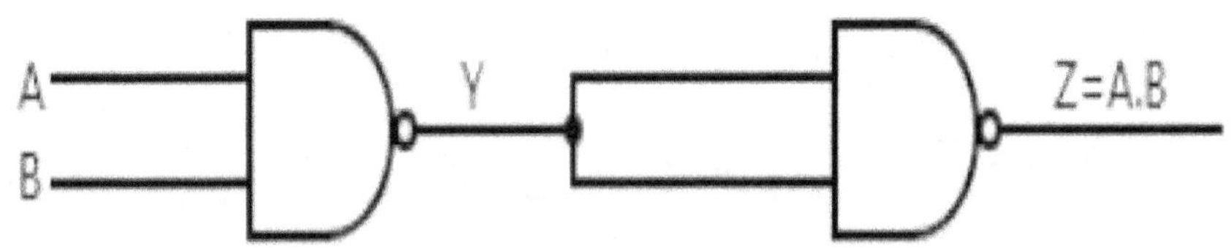

$$Y=(A*B)'=(A*B)''=A*B$$

3.6.5 *OR GATE USING NAND GATE*

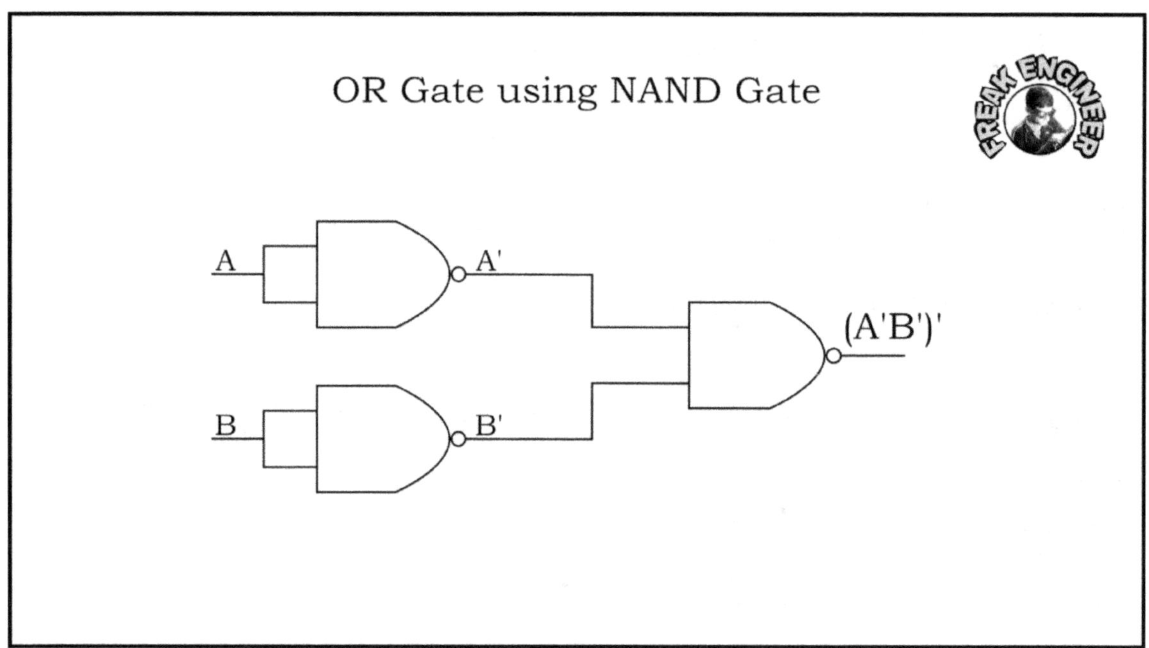

$Y=(A'*B')'=A+B$

3.6.6 *NOT GATE USING NAND GATE*

Truth Table

A (Input)	B (Input)	$Y = \overline{(AB)} = \overline{A}$
0	0	1
1	1	0

3.6.7 *XOR GATE USING NAND GATE*

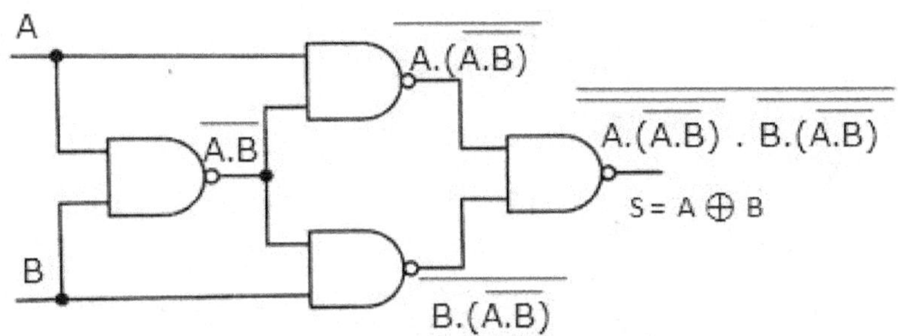

3.6.8 *X-NOR GATE USING NAND GATE*

NAND Gates as EX-NOR Gate

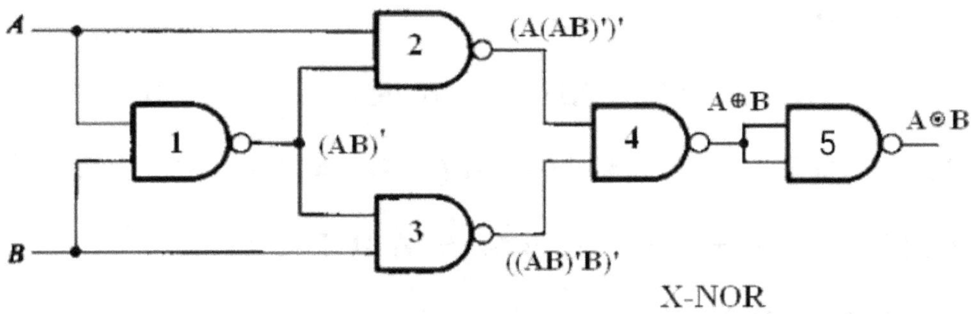

3.6.9 *X-NOR GATE USING NOR GATE*

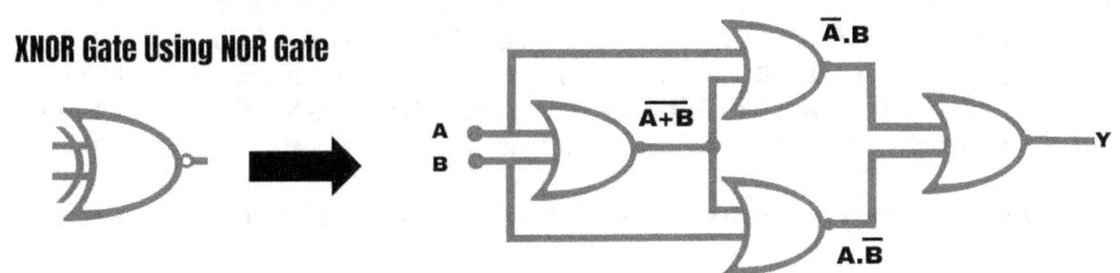

$$Y=((A'*B)+(A*B'))'=A*B+A'*B'$$

3.6.10 *X-OR GATE USING NOR GATE*

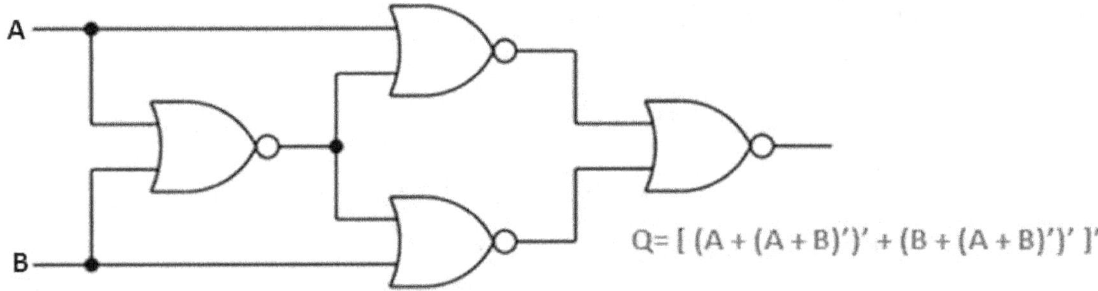

3.7 SOME EXAMPLES OF BOOLEAN ALGEBRA:

1. ((xyz+x'y')'+yz)'= (xyz+x'y').(y'+z') = xyy'z+ xyzz' +x'y'y' +x'y'z'

= x'y'z'+ x'y'=x'y'.(1+z')=x'y'   [yy'=zz'=0; 1+z'=1]

2. (A+B).(A+B').(A'C)=(A+AB'+AB+BB').(A'+C)=(A+AB+AB').(A'+C)

=AA'+AA'B'+AA'B+AC+ABC+AB'C=AC.(1+B)+AB'C=AC.(1+B')=AC

[1+B=1+B'=1]

3. A+A'B+(A+B)'.C+(A+B+C)'.D=A+A'B+A'B'C+A'B'C'D

=A+A'B+A'B'.(C+C'D)=A+A'B++A'B'(C+D)=A+B+A'B'C+A'B'D

=(A+A').(A+B'C)+(B+B').(B+A'D)=A+B+A'D+B'C

=(A+A').(A+D)+(B+B').(B+D)=A+B+C+D

CHAPTER-4

DIGITAL LOGIC CODE CONVERTER (Binary to gray code converter)

Here in this chapter we will one special application of digital logic code ; the name of the code is grey code ; sometimes this code is called reflected code due to single bit change. Here in this chapter we will see binary to grey code conversion along-with design of binary to grey code converter. But here we use KAGNUZEN-MAP or K-map in every step of our problem so we need to know the procedure of k-map;

1. Loop size must be maximum 2 or 2^n number of logic 1 should be taken in a single loop

2. **Don't care term must be avoided as much as possible; here we use 2 bit, 3 bit or 4 bit K-MAP as per our requirements.**

4.1 *BINARY TO GARY CODE CONVERSION*

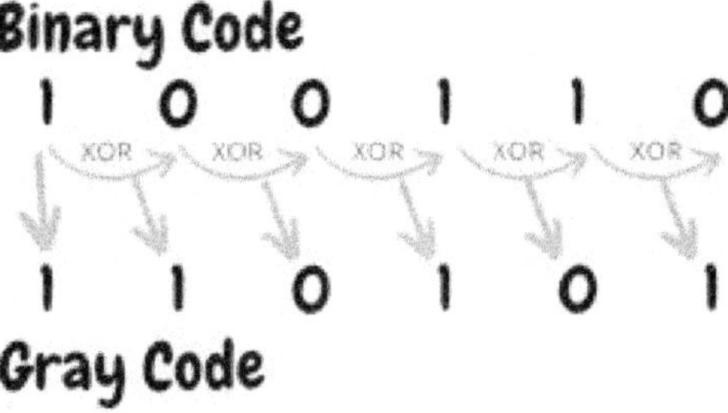

4.2 GRAY TO BINARY CODE CONVERSION

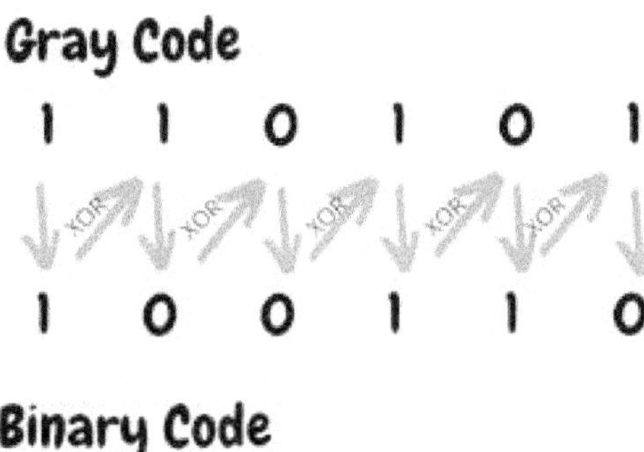

4.3 *BINARY TO GRAY CODE CONVERTER*

BINARY CODE				GRAY CODE			
A	B	C	D	A_1	B_1	C_1	D_1
0	0	0	0	0	0	0	0
0	0	0	1	0	0	0	1
0	0	1	0	0	0	1	1
0	0	1	1	0	0	1	0
0	1	0	0	0	1	1	0
0	1	0	1	0	1	1	1
0	1	1	0	0	1	0	1
0	1	1	1	0	1	0	0
1	0	0	0	1	1	0	0
1	0	0	1	1	1	0	1

1	0	1	0	1	1	1	1
1	0	1	1	1	1	1	0
1	1	0	0	1	0	1	0
1	1	0	1	1	0	1	1
1	1	1	0	1	0	0	1
1	1	1	1	1	0	0	0
FUNCTION(A,B,C,D)							

A_1

	00	01	11	10
00				
01				
11	1	1	1	1
10	1	1	1	1

$A_1 = A$

A_2

	00	01	11	10
00			1	1
01	1	1		
11	1	1		
10			1	1

$A_2 = B*C^{/} + B^{/}*C$

A_3

	00	01	11	10
00				
01	1	1	1	1
11				
10	1	1	1	1

$A_3 = A*B^{/} + A^{/}*B$

A_4

	00	01	11	10
00		1		1
01		1		1
11		1		1

10		1		1

$A_3 = C*D^/ + C^/$

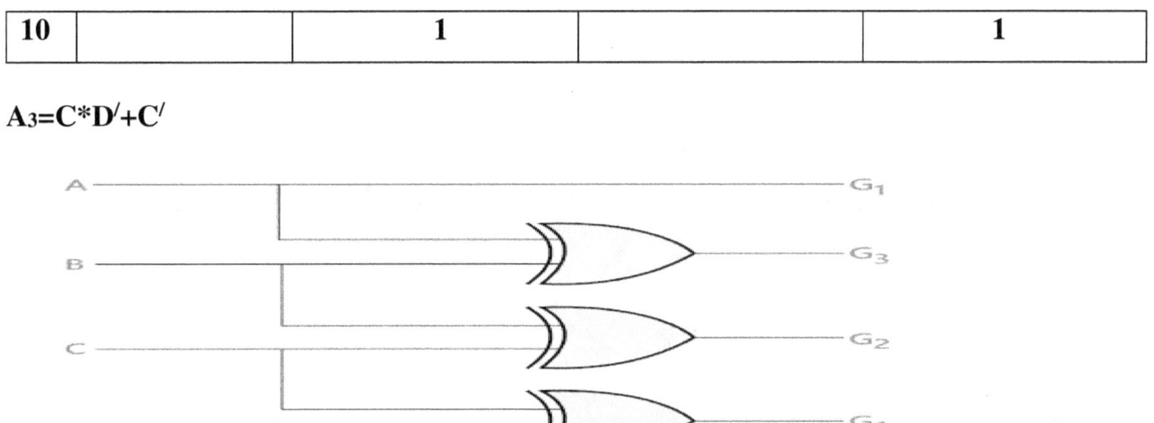

Logic Circuit for Binary to Gray Code Converter

APPLICATION OF ELECTRONIC CIRCUIT DESIGN IN DIGITAL ELECTRONIC CIRCUIT

INTRODUCTION

Here in this chapter we are basically focusing on the construction of digital logic circuit circuits design. Actually in digital electronics there are two types of logic circuits are there , but in order to understand the logic circuits we need to learn a fundamental terminology of digital logic design that is called truth table. Now one by one we will discuss the terminologies related digital electronic circuit design technology.

1. **ARITHMATIC LOGIC CIRCUIT**: Arithmetic logic circuits are the logic circuits which perform arithmetic operations like addition, subtraction in digital computers. Half adder: It is a combinational logic circuit which performs the addition of two bits resulting in two outputs - Sum and Carry. Block diagram of half adder.

2. **COMBINATINAL LOGIC CIRCUIT**: A combinational logic circuit is a circuit whose outputs only depend on the current state of its inputs. These circuits realize Boolean functions and deal with digitized signals, usually denoted by 0s and 1s.

3. **TRUTH TABLE**: A truth table normally consists of rows representing all conceivable input combinations, columns representing the inputs, and columns indicating the output(s). The number of potential input combinations, which is equal to 2 raised to the power of the number of input variables, determines the number of rows in a truth table. Each row represents a particular set of inputs, and the output column lists the output that will be produced from that set of input.

CHAPTER-5

EXAMPLES OF ARITHMATIC LOGIC CIRCUIT

5.1HALF ADDER WITH CIRCUIT

A	B	SUM	CARRY
0	0	0	0
0	1	1	0
1	0	1	0
1	1	0	1

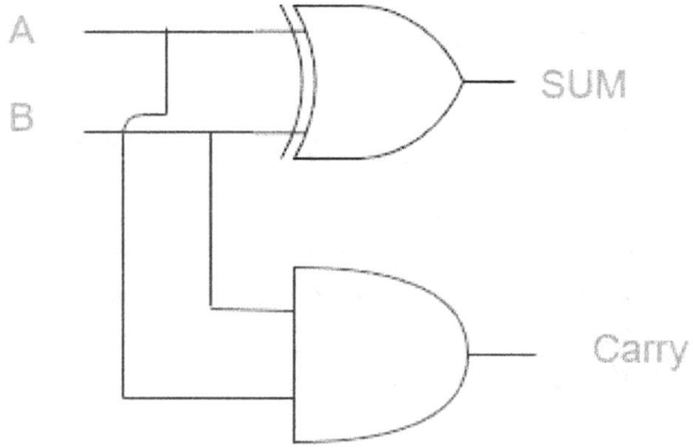

f(A,B) [K-MAP OF SUM AND CARRY OF HALF ADDER]

		SUM		CARRY	
	0	1	0	1	
0	0	1	0	1	
1	0	1	1	1	

SUM=A*B$^{/}$+A$^{/}$*B   **CARRY=A*B**

5.2 HALF SUBSTACTOR WITH CIRCUIT

A	B	DIFF	BORROW
0	0	0	0
0	1	1	1
1	0	1	0
1	1	0	0

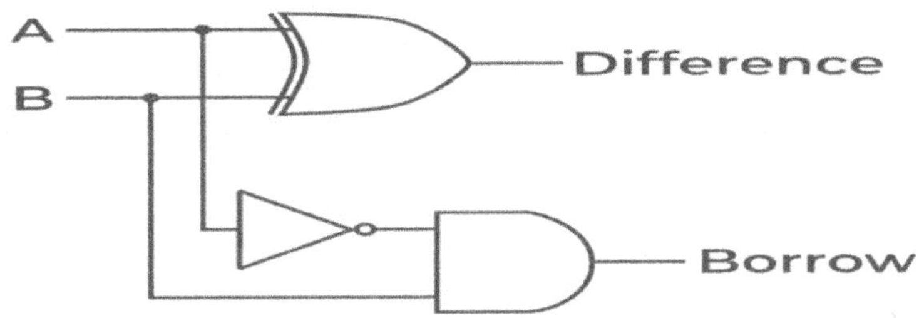

f(A,B)   [K-MAP OF DIFFERENCE AND BORROW OF HALF SUBSTRACTOR]

		DIFF		BORROW	
	0	**1**	**0**	**0**	**1**
0	**0**	**1**	**0**	**0**	**1**
1	**0**	**1**	**1**	**1**	**1**

DIFF=A$^/$*B+A*B$^/$ **BORROW=A$^/$*B**

5.3 *FULL ADDER*

A	B	C	SUM	CARRY
0	0	0	0	0
0	0	1	1	0
0	1	0	1	0
0	1	1	0	1
1	0	0	1	0
1	0	1	0	1
1	1	0	0	1
1	1	1	1	1

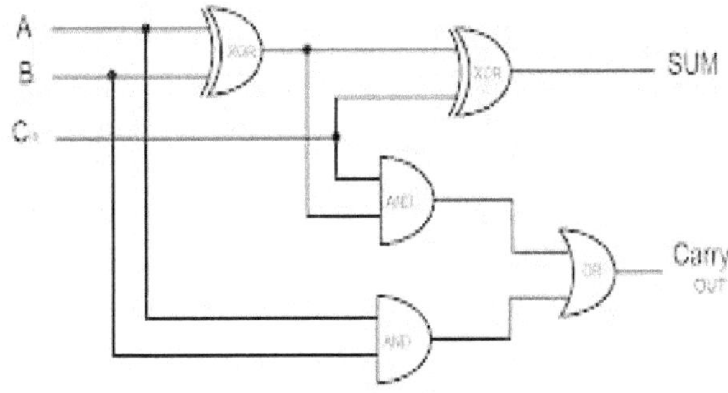

[K-MAP OF SUM AND CARRY OF FULL ADDER]

SUM(A,B,C)

	00	01	11	10
0		1		1
1	1		1	

SUM-= A(+)B(+)C

CARRY(A,B,C)

	00	01	11	10
0			1	
1		1	1	1

CARRY=A*B+B*C+C*A

CHAPTER-6

EXAMPLE OF COMBINATIONAL LOGIC CIRCUIT

(MUX AND DECODER)

6.1 MULTIPLEXER WITH APPLICATIONS:

The word "multiplexor" denotes "**to create multitude**", or "a thing which multiplies". In electrical engineering, multiplexing means to combine several signals in such a way that they can be carried over a single transmission medium. Multiplexer is available in 2^n*1 format for example 2:1 mux, 4:1 mux ,8:1 mux; 16:1 mux. Number of select line for mux is $\log_2(N)$ N=number of inputs

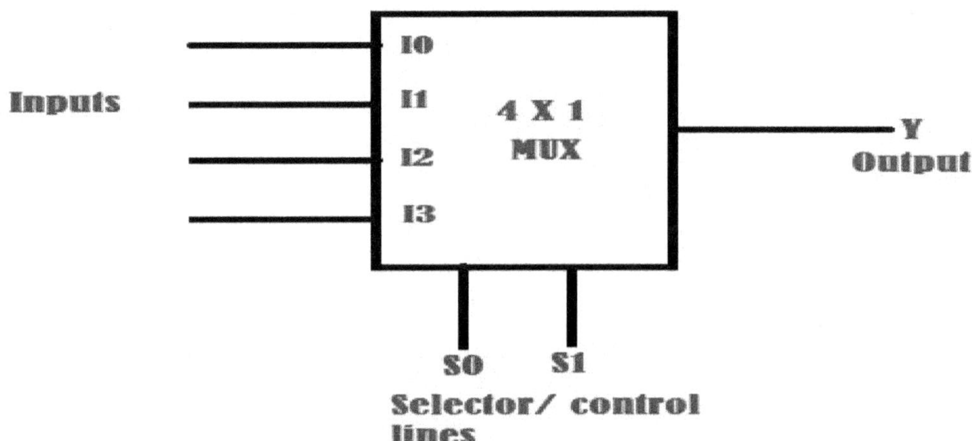

[**NOTE FOR HALF ADDER:** In case of half adder we have two inputs means $2^2=4$ combinations, so we have used 2:1 mux , that means 1 select line ; truth table is same for

half adder for sum and carry. Now according to truth table we have designed sum and carry function for half adder.]

A	B	SUM	CARRY
0	0	0	0
0	1	1	0
1	0	1	0
1	1	0	1

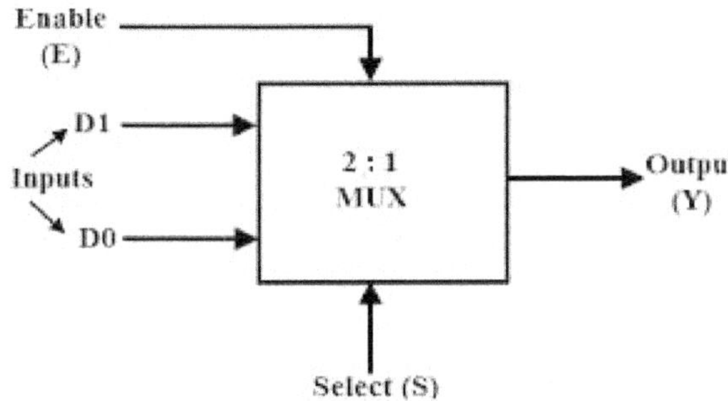

6.2.2 HALF ADDER SUM

	I_0	I_1
A'	0	1
A	2	3
	A	A'

6.2.3 HALF ADDER CARRY

	I_0	I_1
A'	0	1
A	2	3
	A	A'

[NOTE FOR FULL ADDER: In case of full adder we have two inputs means $2^3=8$ combinations, so we have used 4:1 mux , that means 2 select line ; truth table is same for half adder for sum and carry. Now according to truth table we have designed sum and carry function for half adder.]

A	B	C	SUM	CARRY
0	0	0	0	0
0	0	1	1	0
0	1	0	1	0

0	1	1	0	1
1	0	0	1	0
1	0	1	0	1
1	1	0	0	1
1	1	1	1	1

6.2.4 FULL ADDER SUM

	I_0	I_1	I_3	I_4
A'	0	1	2	3
A	4	5	6	7
	A	A'	A'	A

6.2.5 FULL ADDER CARRY

	I_0	I_1	I_3	I_4
A'	0	1	2	3
A	4	5	6	7
	0	A	A	1

6.2.6 2 BIT COMPARATOR

A_1 A_0 B_0 B_1	A>B	A=B	A<B
0 0 0 0	0	1	0
0 0 0 1	0	0	1
0 0 1 0	0	0	1
0 0 1 1	0	0	1
0 1 0 0	1	0	0
0 1 0 1	0	1	0
0 1 1 0	0	0	1
0 1 1 1	0	0	1
1 0 0 0	1	0	0
1 0 0 1	1	0	0

1	0	1	0		0		1		0
1	0	1	1		0		0		1
1	1	0	0		1		0		0
1	1	0	1		1		0		0
1	1	1	0		1		0		0
1	1	1	1		0		1		0

A_1

	00	01	11	10
00				
01	1			
11	1	1		1
10	1	1		

$A_1 = B'_1 B_0' + A_1 A_0 B_0' + A_1 B_1'$

A_2

	00	01	11	10
00		1	1	1
01			1	1
11				
10			1	

$A_2 = A'_1 B_1 + A'_1 A_0' B_0 + A'_0 B_1 B_0$

A_3

	00	01	11	10
00	1			
01		1		
11			1	
10				1

$A_3 = A_1' A_0' B'_1 B_0' + A_1' A_0 B_1' B_0 + A_1 A'_0 B_0' B_1 + A_1 A_0 B_1$

CHAPTER-7

1'S COMPLEMENT AND 2'S COMPLEMENT

The 1's complement of a binary number is obtained by inverting all its bits. The 2's complement of a binary number is obtained by adding 1 to the 1's complement of the number.

1's COMPLEMENT OF 1100

$(1-1)*(1-1)*(1-0)*(1-0)=0011$

2's COMPLEMENT OF 1100

1'S COMPLEMENT +1

$0011+0001=0100$

NOW 2'S COMPLEMENT OF 0100

$(1-0)*(1-1)*(1-0)*(1-0) + 0001= 1100$

Two's complement of a two's complemented digit will be the original binary digit itself.

CHAPTER-8

FLIP-FLOP CONSTRUCTION WITH WORKING PRINCIPLE AND TRUTH TABLE

8.1 WHAT IS RS FLIP FLOP

RS Flip Flop, also known as Reset-Set Flip Flop, is **a fundamental digital storage device that can store one bit of information**. In simpler words, an RS Flip Flop is a logical circuit with two inputs, R (Reset) and S (Set) and two outputs, Q and (inverse of Q).

8.2 TRUTH TABLE OF RS FLIP FLOP

Sl no.	Clock	S	R	Q_{n+1}
1	0	X	X	Q_n
2	1	0	0	No change

Sl no.	Clock	S	R	Qn+1
3	1	0	1	0
4	1	1	0	1
5	1	1	1	Undefined / Forbidden stat

8.3 WHAT IS JK FLIP FLOP

It is one kind of sequential logic circuit which stores binary information in bitwise manner. It consists of two inputs and two outputs. Inputs are Set(J) & Reset(K) and their corresponding outputs are Q and Q'. JK flipflop has two modes of operation which are synchronous mode and asynchronous mode. In synchronous mode, the state will be changed with the clock(clk) signal, and in asynchronous mode, the change of state is independent from its clock signal. Let's see its diagram structure.

8.4 TRUTH TABLE OF JK FLIP FLOP

Clock	J	K	Q_{n+1}	State
0	X	X	Q_n	
1	0	0	Q_n	Hold
1	0	1	0	Reset
1	1	1	1	Set
1	1	1	$\overline{Q_n}$	Toggle

8.5 WHAT IS D FLIP FLOP:

D flip flop is an electronic devices that is known as "delay flip flop" or "data flip flop" which is used to store single bit of data.D flip flops are synchronous or asynchronous. The clock single required for the synchronous version of D flip flops but not for the asynchronous one.The D flip flop has two inputs, data and clock input which controls the flip flop. when clock input is high, the data is transferred to the output of the flip flop and when the clock input is low, the output of the flip flop is held in its previous state.

8.7 TRUTH TABLE OF D FLIP FLOP

Clock	D	Q	Q'	Description
↓ » 0	X	Q	Q'	Memory no change
↑ » 1	0	0	1	Reset Q » 0
↑ » 1	1	1	0	Set Q » 1

8.8 RS FLIP FLOP DIAGRAM BY NAND OR NOR GATE:

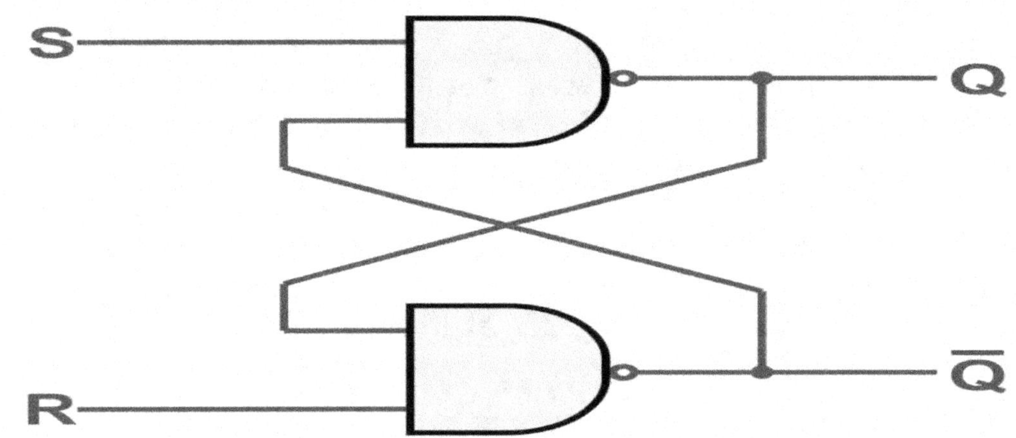

Fig 5.5(a)Wiring an R-S flip-flop using NAND gates

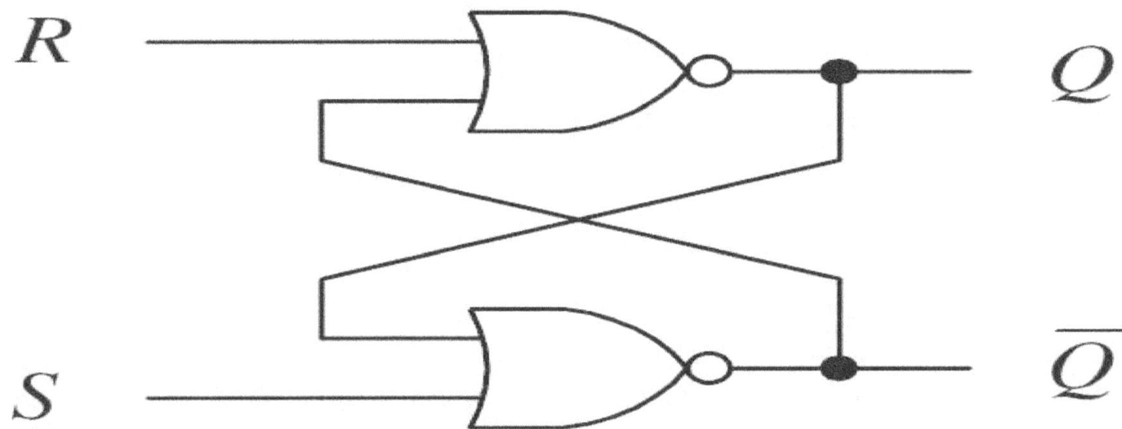

SR FLIP FLOP BY NOR GATE

8.9 JK FLIP FLOP DIAGRAM BY NAND GATE:

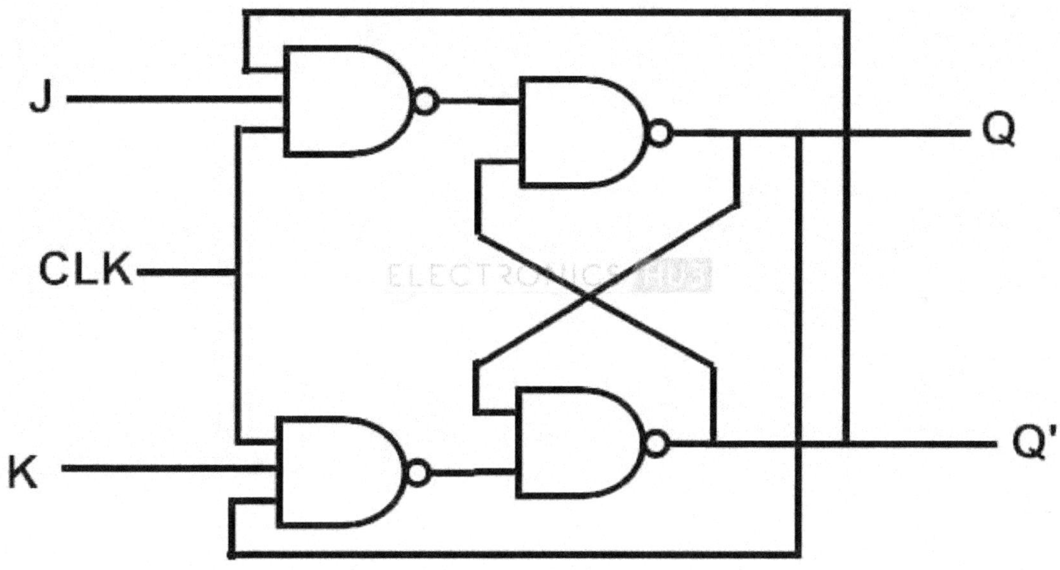

CHAPTER-9

FLIP FLOP CONVERSION

9.1 STATE TRANSITION TABLE OF JK, SR, D FLIP FLOP:

Here author has displayed the state transition table of JK, SR,D flip flop with the help of previously mentioned truth table of corresponding flip-flops:

J K Q_n -> Q_{n+1}

0 0 0 -> 0

0 0 1 -> 1

0 1 0 -> 0

0 1 1 -> 0

1 0 0 -> 1

1 0 1 -> 1

S	R	$Q_n \rightarrow Q_{n+1}$
1	1	0 -> 1
1	1	1 -> 0
0	0	0 -> 0
0	0	1 -> 1
0	1	0 -> 0
0	1	1 -> 0
1	0	0 -> 1
1	0	1 -> 1

$Q_n \rightarrow Q_{n+1}$	S	R	D	J	K
0 -> 0	0	X	0	0	X
0 -> 1	1	0	1	1	X
1 -> 0	0	1	0	X	1
1 -> 1	X	0	1	X	0

9.2 CONVERSION JK TO SR

S	R	$Q_n \rightarrow Q_{n+1}$	J	K
0	0	0 -> 0	0	X
0	1	0 -> 0	0	X
1	0	0 -> 1	1	X
0	0	1 -> 1	X	0
0	1	1 -> 0	X	1
1	0	1 -> 1	X	0

J(Q$_n$,S.R)

	00	01	11	10
0			X	1
1	X	X	X	X

J=S

K(Q$_n$,S.R)

	00	01	11	10
0	X	X	X	X
1		1	X	

K=R

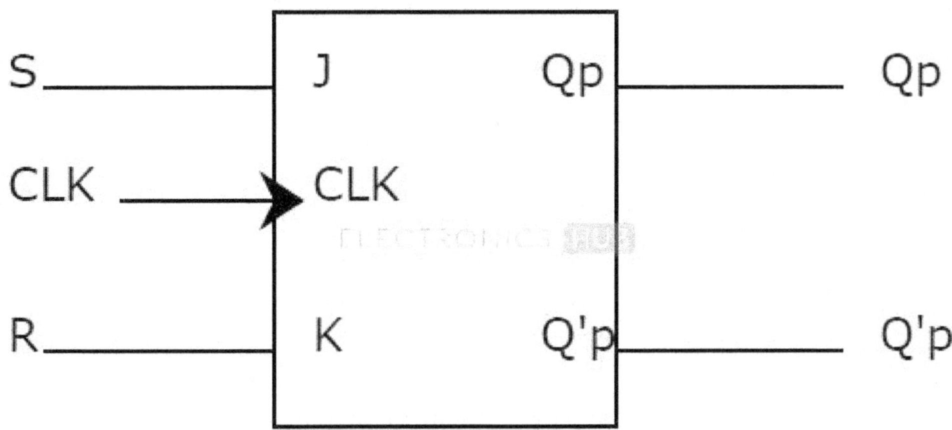

9.3 CHARACTERISTICS OF SR FLIP-FLOP

S R   Q$_n$->Q$_{n+1}$

0 0   0-> 0

0 1   0-> 0

1 0   0-> 1

0 0   1-> 1

0 1   1-> 0

1 0   1-> 1

<u>L(Q_n ,S.R)</u>

	00	01	11	10
0			X	1
1	1		X	1

L=S+Q_nR'

9.4 CHARACTERISTICS OF JK FLIP-FLOP

J K Q_n->Q_{n+1}

0 0 0->0

0 1 0->0

1 0 0->1

1 1 0->1

0 0 1->1

0 1 1->0

1 0 1->1

1 1 1->0

<u>L(Q_n ,,J.K)</u>

	00	01	11	10
0			1	1
1	1			1

L=Q_n' J+Q_nK'

9.5 CONVERSION SR TO JK

J K Q_n-> Q_{n+1} S R

0 0 0-> 0   0 X

0 1 0-> 0   0 X

1 0 0-> 1   1 0

1 1 0-> 1   1 0

0 0 1-> 1   X 0

0   1   1-> 0   0   1

1   0   1-> 1   X   0

1   1   1-> 0   0   1

$S(Q_n, J.K)$

	00	01	11	10
0			1	1
1	X			X

$S=Q_n'J$

$R(Q_n, J.K)$

	00	01	11	10
0	X	X		
1		1	1	

$R=Q_nK$

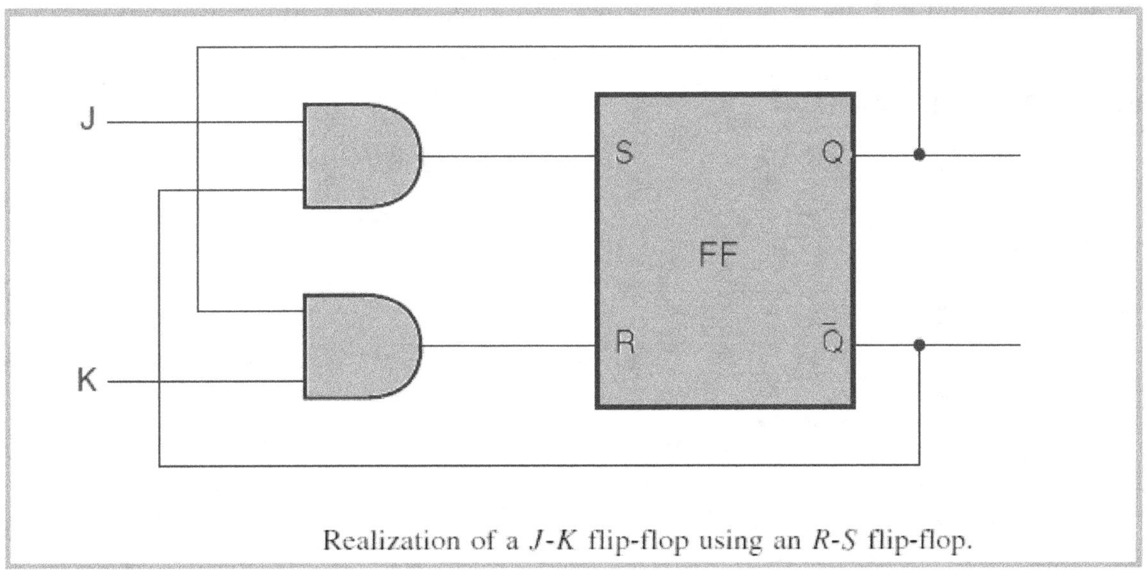

Realization of a *J-K* flip-flop using an *R-S* flip-flop.

9.7 CONVERSION D TO SR

S   R Q_n-> Q_{n+1} J

0   0   0-> 0   0

0   1   0-> 0   0

1   0   0-> 1   1

0   0   1-> 1   1

0   1   1-> 0   0

1   0   1-> 1   1

$\underline{D(Q_n, S.R)}$

	00	01	11	10
0			X	1
1	1		X	1

$D = S + Q_n R'$

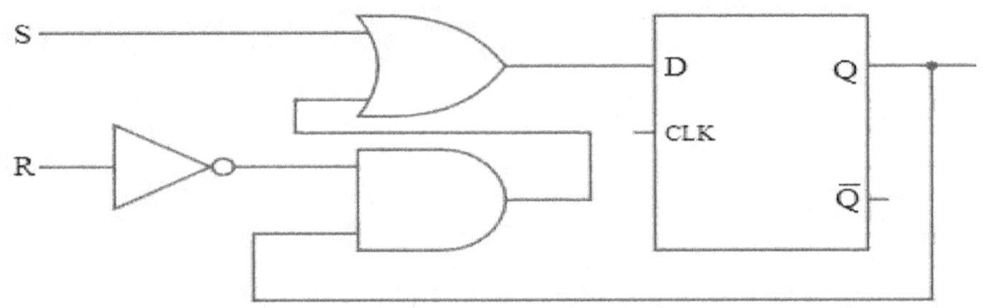

9.8 CONVERSION SR TO D

D	$Q_n \to Q_{n+1}$	S	R
0	0-> 0	0	X
1	0-> 1	1	0
0	0-> 0	0	X
1	0-> 1	1	0
0	1-> 0	0	1
1	1-> 1	X	0
0	1-> 0	0	1
1	1-> 1	X	0

<u>S(Q$_n$,D)</u>

	0	1
0		1
1		X

S=D

<u>R(Q$_n$,D)</u>

	0	1
0	1	
1	X	

R=D'

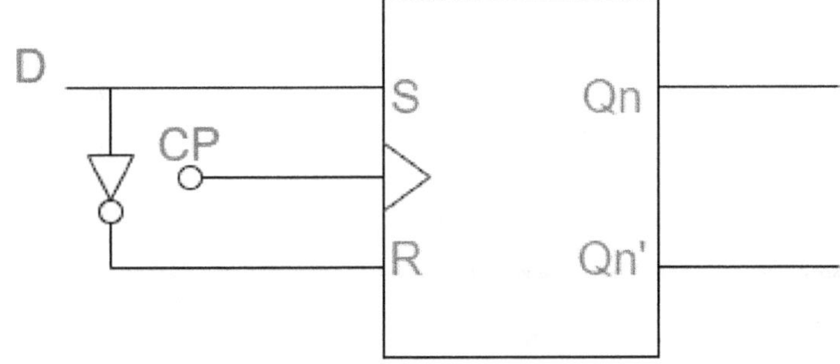

9.9 CONVERSION D TO JK

J	K	Q$_n$-> Q$_{n+1}$	D
0	0	0-> 0	0
0	1	0-> 0	0
1	0	0-> 1	1
1	1	0-> 1	1
0	0	1-> 1	1
0	1	1-> 0	0
1	0	1-> 1	1
1	1	1-> 0	0

<u>D(Q_n,J.K)</u>

	00	01	11	10
0			1	1
1	1			1

$D = Q_n' j + Q_n K'$

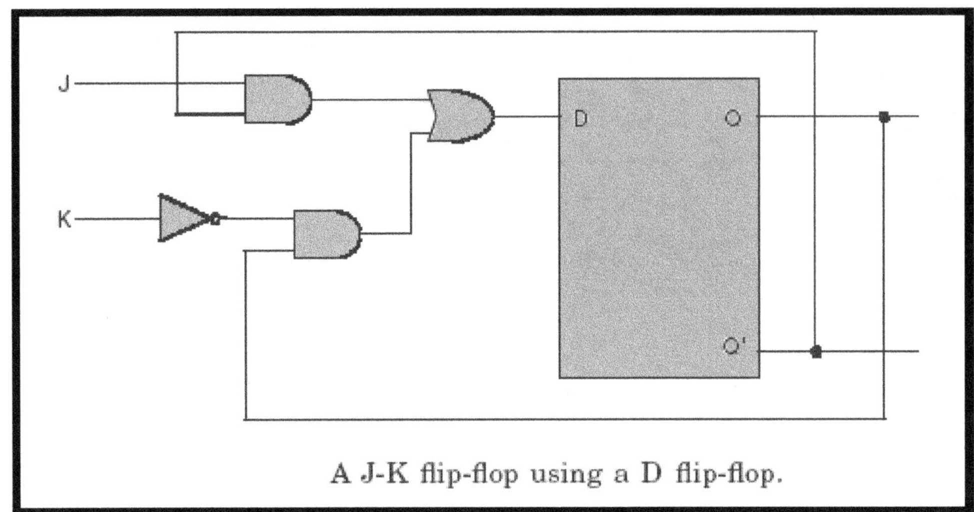

A J-K flip-flop using a D flip-flop.

9.10 CONVERSION JK TO D

D	Q_n-> Q_{n+1}	J	K
0	0-> 0	0	X
1	0-> 1	1	X
0	0-> 0	0	X
1	0-> 1	1	X
0	1-> 0	X	1
1	1-> 1	X	0
0	1-> 0	X	1
1	1-> 1	X	0

<u>J(Q_n,D)</u>

	0	1
0		1
1	X	X

J=D

K(Q_n ,D)

	0	**1**
0	**X**	**X**
1	**1**	

K=D$'$

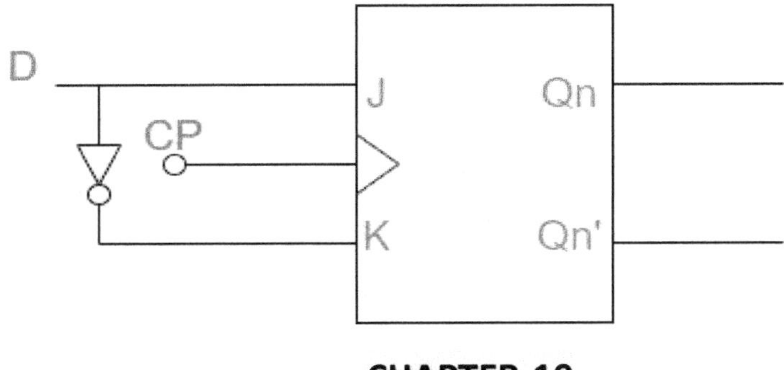

CHAPTER-10

COUNTER AND REGISTER

10.1 WHAT IS COUNTER IN DIGITAL ELECTRONICS

A counter in digital electronics is a sequential logic circuit that goes through a predetermined sequence of states upon the application of input pulses. Counters can be broadly classified into two categories based on their operation: synchronous counters and asynchronous counters.

10.2 WHAT IS TIMING DIAGRAM OF COUNTER IN DIGITAL ELECTRONICS

A digital timing diagram represents a set of signals in the time domain. A timing diagram can contain many rows, usually one of them being the clock. It is a tool commonly used in digital electronics, hardware debugging, and digital communications.

10.3 UP COUNTER [an example of down counter 3 bit]

000->001->010->011->100->101->110->111

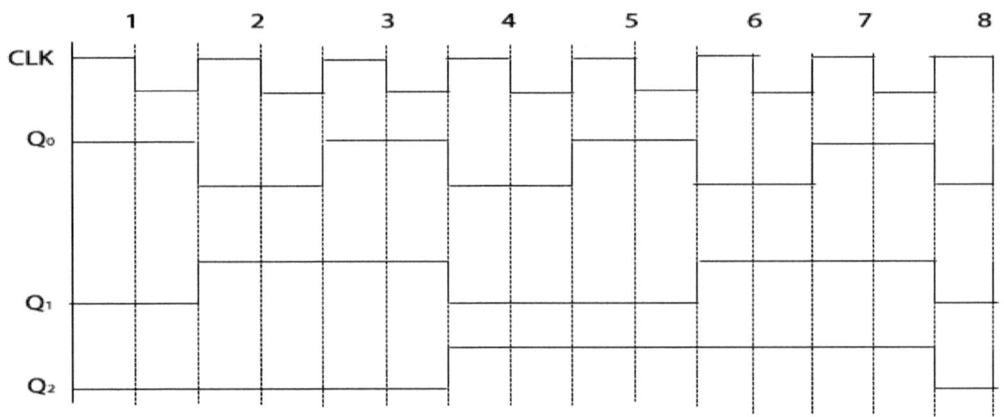

10.4 DOWN COUNTER [an example of mod 3 down counter]

111->110->101->100->011->010->001->000

3 bit or Mod 8
Down counter

When M= 1

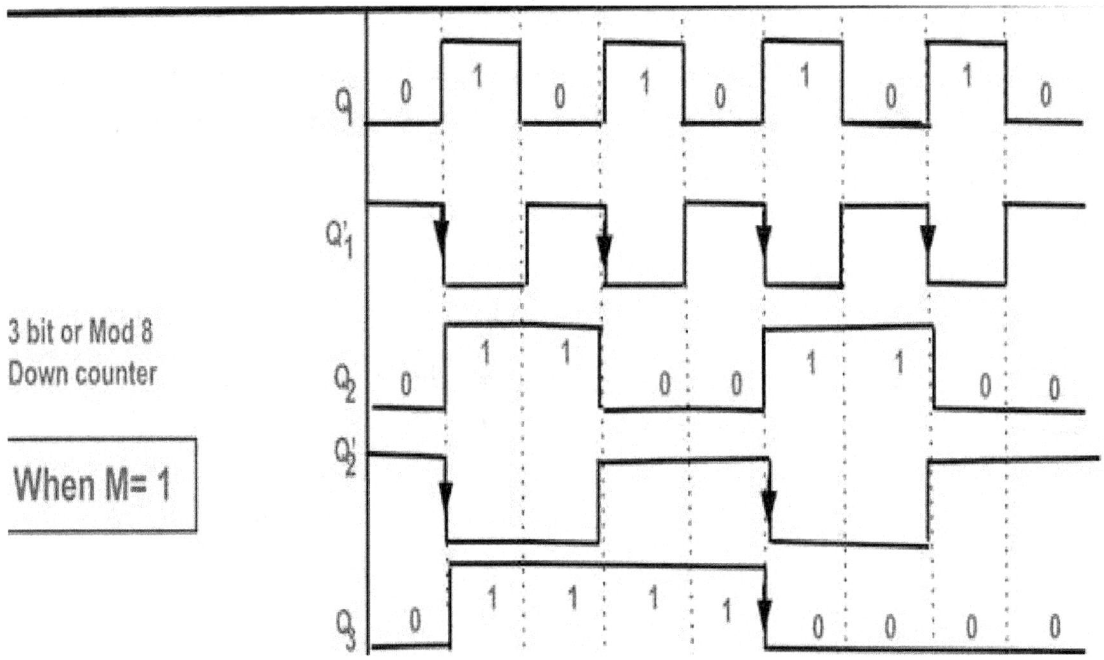

10.4 CIRCUIT DIAGRAM OF 3-BIT UP COUNTER

Logic Diagram for 3- bit Up Counter:

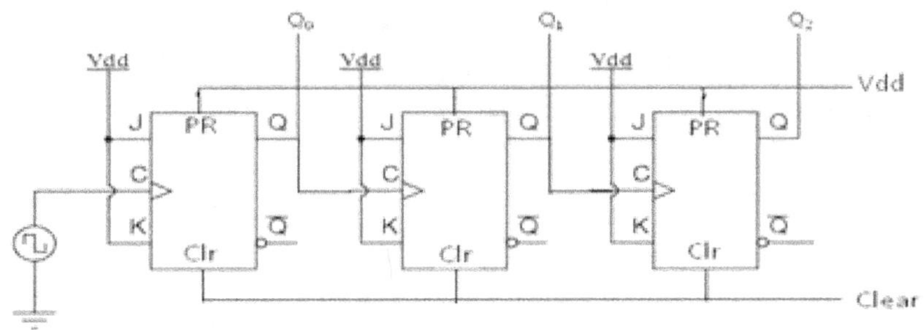

10.5 CIRCUIT DIAGRAM OF 3-BIT DOWN COUNTER

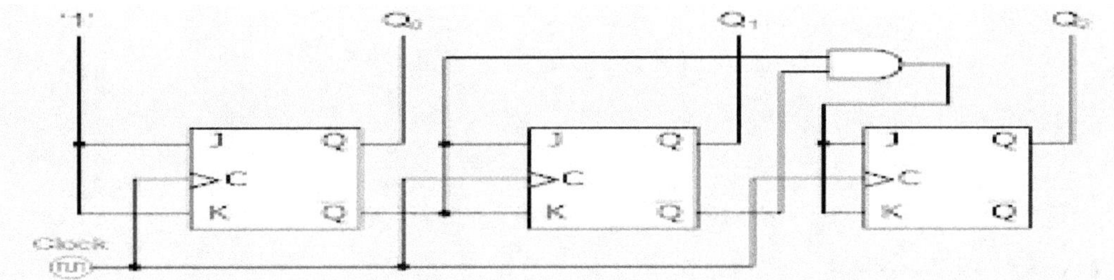

10.6 WHAT IS TRIGARRING OF CLOCK PULSE IN COUNTER

Clock pulse triggering determines when a sequential circuit responds to input changes. There are four types of clock triggering, including edge triggering and level triggering.

There are two types of triggering of clock pulse in digital electronics.

10.6.1 EDGE TRIGGERING

a. Positive edge triggering

Occurs when the output responds to input changes only at the rising edge of the clock pulse. This is also called rising edge triggering.

b. Negative Edge triggering

Common in synchronous circuits like counters, edge triggering updates the output state based on the falling edge of a clock pulse.

10.6.2 LEVEL TRIGGERING

a. Positive level triggering

When there is a transition from 0 to 1 it is named as positive edge level triggered.

b.Negative level triggering

when the clock pulse makes a transition from high to low i.e. from 1 to 0 it is termed as negative edge triggered.

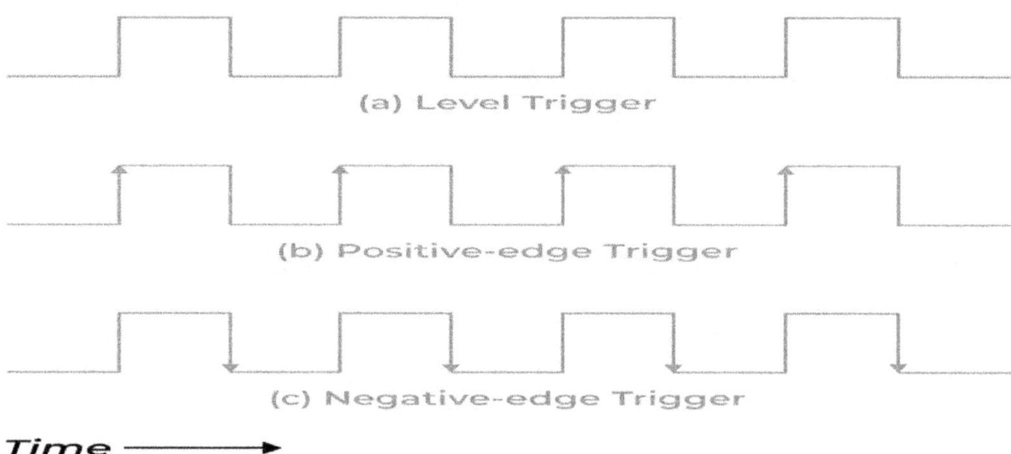

10.6.3 BINARY TO GREY COUNTER DESIGN

One example of digital counter design has been displayed in the below example; in order to understand that we need to learn binary to grey code conversion example;

BINARY				GREY		
Q_2	Q_1	Q_0		Q_2	Q_1	Q_0
0	0	0		0	0	0
0	0	1		0	0	1
0	1	0		0	1	1
0	1	1		0	1	0
1	0	0		1	1	0
1	0	1		1	1	1

1	1	0	1	0	1
1	1	1	1	0	0

So our binary sequence of the counter will be

$S_0 \to S_1 \to S_3 \to S_2 \to S_6 \to S_7 \to S_5 \to S_4 \to S_0$

Present			Next								
Q_2	Q_1	Q_0	Q_2	Q_1	Q_0	J_2	K_2	J_1	K_1	J_0	K_0
0	0	0	0	0	1	0	X	0	X	1	X
0	0	1	0	1	1	0	X	1	X	X	0
0	1	1	0	1	0	0	X	X	0	X	1
0	1	0	1	1	0	1	X	X	0	0	X
1	1	0	1	1	1	X	0	X	0	1	X
1	1	1	1	0	1	X	0	X	1	X	0
1	0	1	1	0	0	X	0	0	X	X	1
1	0	0	0	0	0	X	1	0	X	0	X

$J_2(Q_2, Q_1.Q_0)$

	00	01	11	10
0				1
1	X	X	X	X

$J_2 = Q_1 Q'_0$

$K_2(Q_2, Q_1.Q_0)$

	00	01	11	10
0	X	X	X	X
1	1			

$K_2 = Q'_1 Q'_0$

$J_1(Q_2, Q_1.Q_0)$

	00	01	11	10
0		1	X	X
1			X	X

$J_1 = Q'_2 Q_0$

$K_1(Q_2, Q_1.Q_0)$

	00	01	11	10
0	X	X		
1	X	X	1	

$K_1 = Q_2 Q_0$

$J_0(Q_2, Q_1.Q_0)$

	00	01	11	10
0	1	X	X	
1		X	X	1

$J_0 = Q_2 Q_1 + Q'_2 Q_1' = xnor(Q_2, Q_1)$

$K_0(Q_2, Q_1.Q_0)$

	00	01	11	10
0	X		1	X
1	X	1		X

$K_0 = Q_2 Q_1' + Q_2' Q_1 = xor(Q_2, Q_1)$

So we have completed the design of the binary to grey counter design sequence now let's design the circuit by using 3 JK flip flops from the above mentioned K-MAPs.

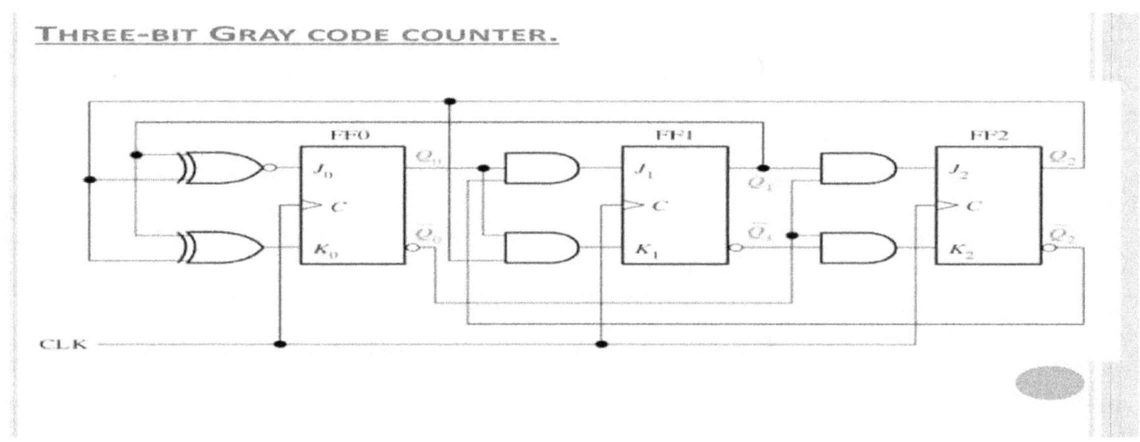

10.7 WHAT IS REGISTER IN DIGITAL-ELECTRONICS:-

Flip flops can be used to store a single bit of binary data (1 or 0). However, in order to store multiple bits of data, we need multiple flip-flops. N flip flops are to be connected in order to store n bits of data. A Register is a device that is used to store such information. It is a group of flip-flops connected in series used to store multiple bits of data. The information stored within these registers can be transferred with the help of shift registers.

10.7.1 TYPES OF REGISTERS IN DIGITAL ELECTRONICS:

a. Serial In Serial Out shift register
   The shift register, which allows serial input (one bit after the other through a single data line) and produces a serial output is known as a Serial-In Serial-Out shift register. Since there is only one output, the data leaves the shift register one bit at a time in a serial pattern, thus the name Serial-In Serial-Out Shift Register. The logic circuit given below shows a serial-in serial-out shift register. The circuit consists of four D flip-flops which are connected in a serial manner. All these flip-flops are synchronous with each other since the same clock signal is applied to each flip-flop.

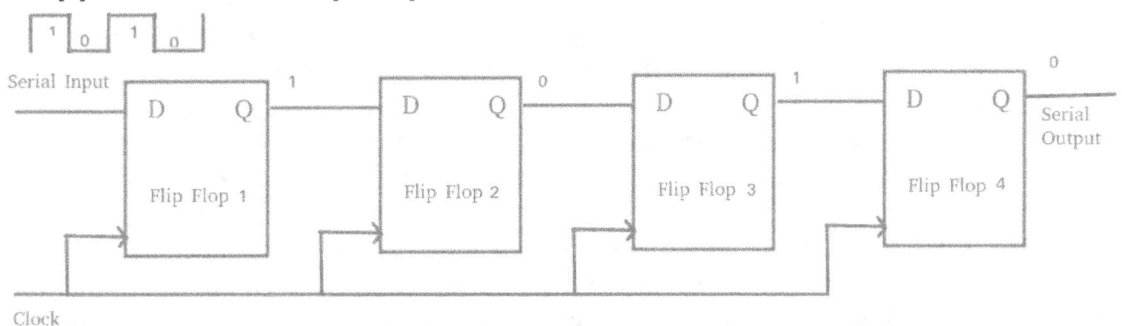

Serial-In Serial-Out Shift Register (SISO)

The above circuit is an example of a shift right register, taking the serial data input from the left side of the flip flop. The main use of a SISO is to act as a delay element.

b. Serial In parallel Out shift register
   The shift register, which allows serial input (one bit after the other through a single data line) and produces a parallel output is known as the Serial-In Parallel-Out shift register. The logic circuit given below shows a serial-in-parallel-out shift register. The circuit consists of four D flip-flops which are connected. The clear (CLR) signal is connected in addition to the clock signal to all 4 flip flops in order to RESET them. The

output of the first flip-flop is connected to the input of the next flip flop and so on. All these flip-flops are synchronous with each other since the same clock signal is applied to each flip-flop.

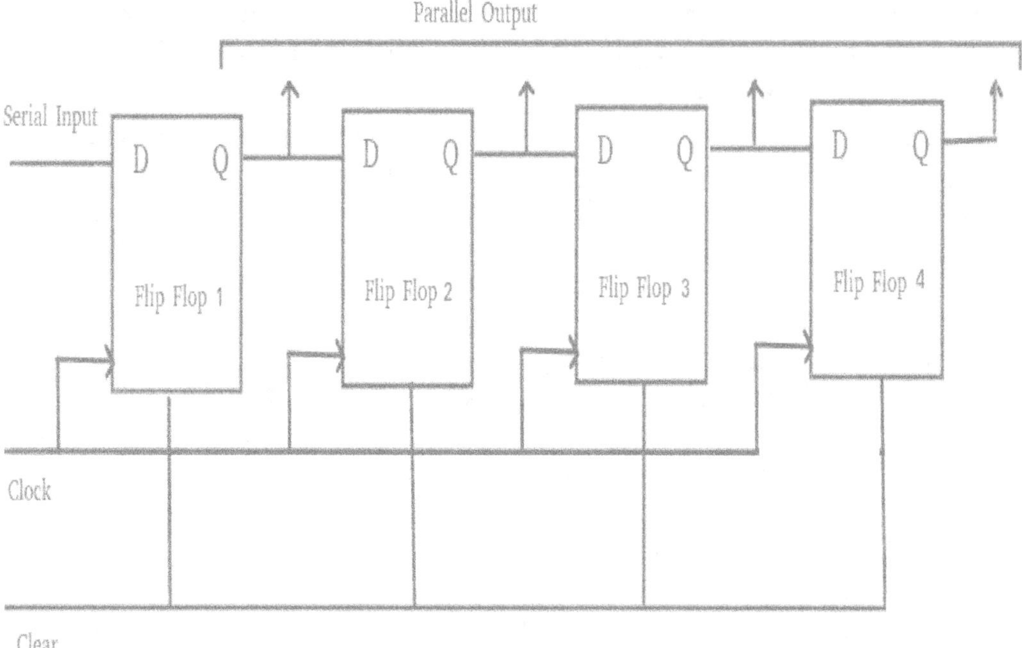

Serial-In Parallel-Out shift Register (SIPO)

The above circuit is an example of a shift right register, taking the serial data input from the left side of the flip-flop and producing a parallel output. They are used in communication lines where de-multiplexing of a data line into several parallel lines is required because the main use of the SIPO register is to convert serial data into parallel data.

c. **Parallel In Serial Out shift register**

The shift register, which allows parallel input (data is given separately to each flip flop and in a simultaneous manner) and produces a serial output is known as a Parallel-In Serial-Out shift register. The logic circuit given below shows a parallel-in-serial-out shift register. The circuit consists of four D flip-flops which are connected. The clock input is directly connected to all the flip-flops but the input data is connected individually to each flip-flop through a multiplexer at the input of every flip-flop. The output of the previous flip-flop and parallel data input are connected to the input of the MUX and the output of MUX is connected to the next flip-flop. All these flip-flops are synchronous with each other since the same clock signal is applied to each flip-flop.

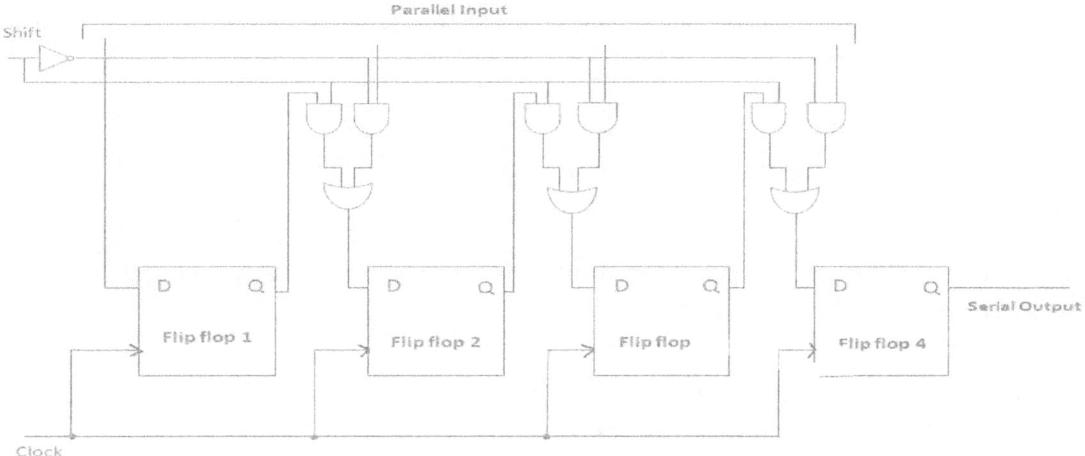

Parallel-In Serial-Out Shift Register (PISO)

A Parallel in Serial Out (PISO) shift register is used to convert parallel data to serial data.

d. Parallel In parallel Out shift register

The shift register, which allows parallel input (data is given separately to each flip flop and in a simultaneous manner) and also produces a parallel output is known as Parallel-In parallel-Out shift register. The logic circuit given below shows a parallel-in-parallel-out shift register. The circuit consists of four D flip-flops which are connected. The clear (CLR) signal and clock signals are connected to all 4 flip-flops. In this type of register, there are no interconnections between the individual flip-flops since no serial shifting of the data is required. Data is given as input separately for each flip flop and in the same way, output is also collected individually from each flip flop.

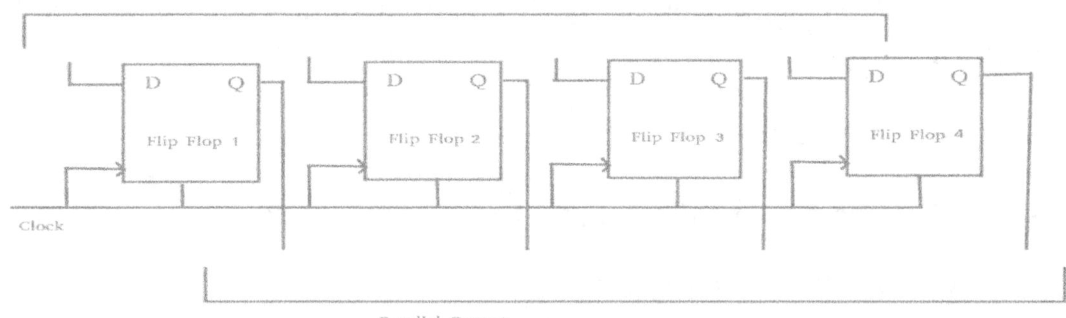

Parallel-In Parallel-Out Shift Register (PIPO)

A Parallel in Parallel out (PIPO) shift register is used as a temporary storage device and like SISO Shift register it acts as a delay element.

CHAPTER-11

LOGIC FAMILIES IN DIGITAL ELECTRONICS

Digital systems are mostly designed by combining various logic functions. All these logic circuits are available in IC modules and are divided into many 'families'. Each family is classified by abbreviations that indicate the type of logic circuit used. They are of the following

1. Resistance-transistor logic(RTL)
2. Diode transistor logic (DTL)
3. Transistor- Transistor logic(TTL)
4. Emitter Coupled logic(ECL)
5. Integrated-Injection logic(I^2C)
6. Complementary metal oxide semiconductor (CMOS) etc

11.1 Bi-polar families

In Bi-polar families there are three basic families,

DTL-> Diode-transistor logic

TTL-> Transistor-transistor logic

ECL-> Emitter-coupled logic

Among all the logic families ECL is the fastest one used in high speed applications.

11.2 MOS families

In MOS category the following families are included

PMOS-> P channel MOSFETS

NMOS-> N channel MOSFETS

CMOS-> Complementary MOSFETS

11.3 Characteristics of a logic families

a. Logic flexibility of a digital IC is a measure of its unity in meeting the various system needs.

b. Connection of gate output terminals together are using them directly to perform additional logic function without any extra hardware.

c. Availability of a complemented output.

d. Capability to drive non-standard loads such as long lines, lamps etc.

e. Input/output facilities.

f. Ability to drive other logic family circuits.

g. Ability to have many types of gates in the same family.

11.4 Voltage and Current families:

a. V_{IH} (min) (High level Input Voltage)- Logical 1 (+5 Volt) of input voltage

b. V_{IL} (max) (Low level Input Voltage)- Logical 0 (+0 Volt) of input voltage

c. V_{OH}(min) (High level Output Voltage)- Output in logical 1 (+5 Volt) state

d. V_{OL}(max) (Low level Output Voltage)- Output in logical 0 (+0 Volt) state

e. I_{IH}(High level input current)- Current which flows into an input when a specified high level voltage

f. I_{IL}(Low level input Current)- Current which flows into an when a low level voltage is applied to the input

g. I_{OH}(High level output Current)- Current that flows from an output in logical 1 state under specified load conditions.

h. I_{OL}(Low level output Current)- Current that flows from an output in logical 0 state under specified load conditions.

i. Fan Out- The maximum number of standard logic inputs that an output can drive reliably is called Fan out.

j. Propagation delay- The delay in between input and output signals is called propagation delay.

k. Noise immunity- The noise immunity of a logic circuit refers to circuits ability to tolerate voltages on its inputs;

High state noise margin- $V_{NH} = V_{OH}(min) - V_{IH}(min)$

Low state noise margin- $V_{NL} = V_{IL}(max) - V_{IH}(max)$

CHAPTER-12

CMOS VLSI GATE DESIGN LOGIC

Complementary metal oxide semiconductor is a technology for constructing integrated circuits. CMOS is used in microprocessors, microcontrollers, static RAM and other digital logic circuits, CMOS technology is also used for several analog circuits such as image sensors, data converters, highly integrated tran-civers for many types of communications. CMOS sometimes referred to as complementary symmetry metal oxide semiconductors. The words complementary symmetry referred to the fact that the typical design style with CMOS uses complementary and symmetrical pairs of P-type and N-type metal oxide semiconductor field effect transistors for logic function. Two important characteristics of CMOS devices are high noise immunity and low static power consumption. Since one transistor of the pair is always off the series combination draws significant power only momentarily during switching between ON and OFF states. Consequently CMOS devices produce as much waste heat as other form of logic for example transistor transistor -transistor logic or NMOS logic. CMOS also allows a high density of logic function on a chip . That's why CMOS became the most used technology to be implemented in VLSI chip.

12.1 Application of CMOS:

1. Designing different types of digital circuit like full adder, half adder, XOR, XNOR, AND NAND , OR , NOR gates.

2. Producing layouts of above mentioned circuits.

3. Designing low power consuming integrated circuits.

12.2 Some cases of design of digital logic gate by using CMOS:

12.2.1 CMOS inverter design by using cmos technology

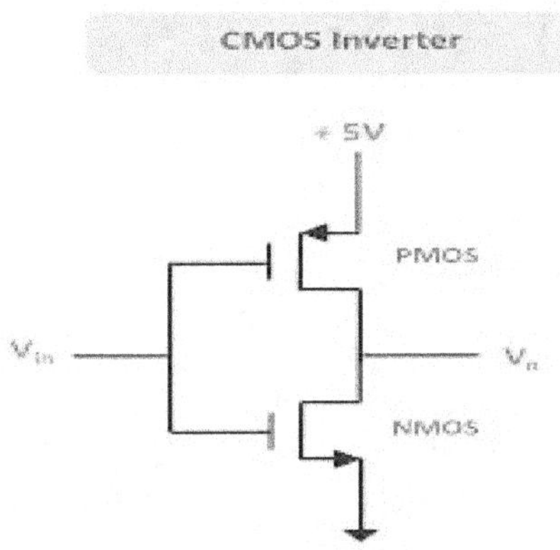

12.2.2 NAND gate design by using CMOS

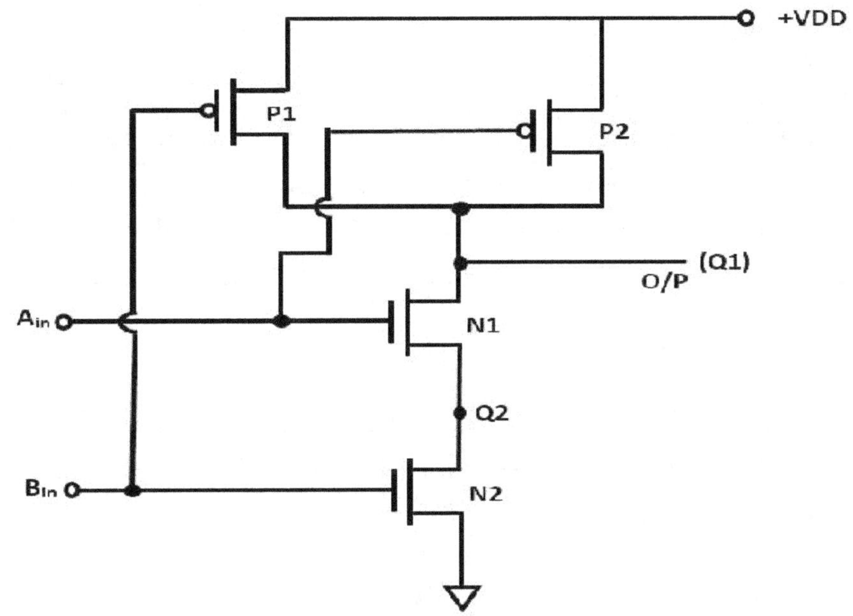

12.2.2 NOR gate design by using CMOS

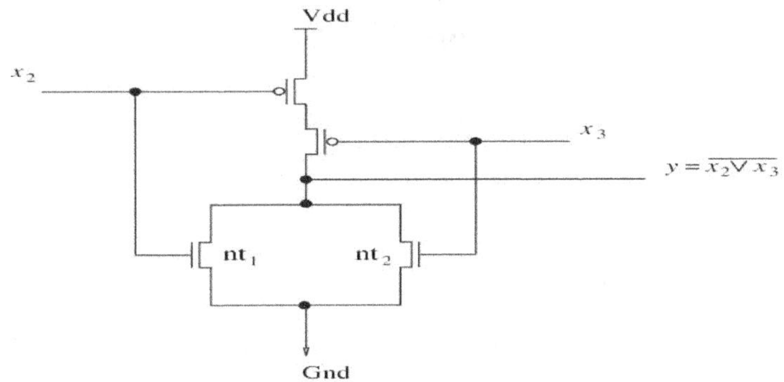

CHAPTER 13

PRGOAMMABLE LOGIC DEVICE

13.1 WHAT IS PROGRAMMABLE LOGIC DEVICE:-

A programmable logic device is a general purpose chip by which logic circuits can be implemented. Basically it contains a collection of logic elements that can be customized in different ways, PLD can thought to be a black box that contains logic gates and programmable switches.

Numerous chips are available in the market in which commonly used logic circuits are used. These chips are called standard chips. Up to 1980 , these types of standard chips were used in different PCBs, the drawback of this kind of chips is that the functionality of chip is fixed and cannot be changed.

13.2 DIFFERENT TYPES OF PLD:-

DIFFERENT TYPES OF PLD	AND GATE	OR GATE
PROGRAMMABLE LOGIC ARRAY	PROGRAMMABLE	PROGRAMMABLE
PROGRAMMABLE ARRAY LOGIC	PROGRAMMABLE	PROGRAMMABLE
FIELD PROGRAMMABLE GATE ARRAY	FIXED	PROGRAMMABLE

13.3 DRAWBACKS OF PLD:-

The drawback of PLD is that it consumes valuable chip area and speed of chip is limited. So to overcome the above difficulties the use of custom or semi-custom chips are being evolved.

13.4 EXPLAIN THE APPLICATION OF PLD:-

Simple PLD's like PLA's and PAL's are used for implementation of small logic circuits. SPLDs offer low cost and high speed. CPLD's are used for implementation of larger circuits having more number od gates.

13.5 STRUCTURE OF DIFFERENT OF PLD:-

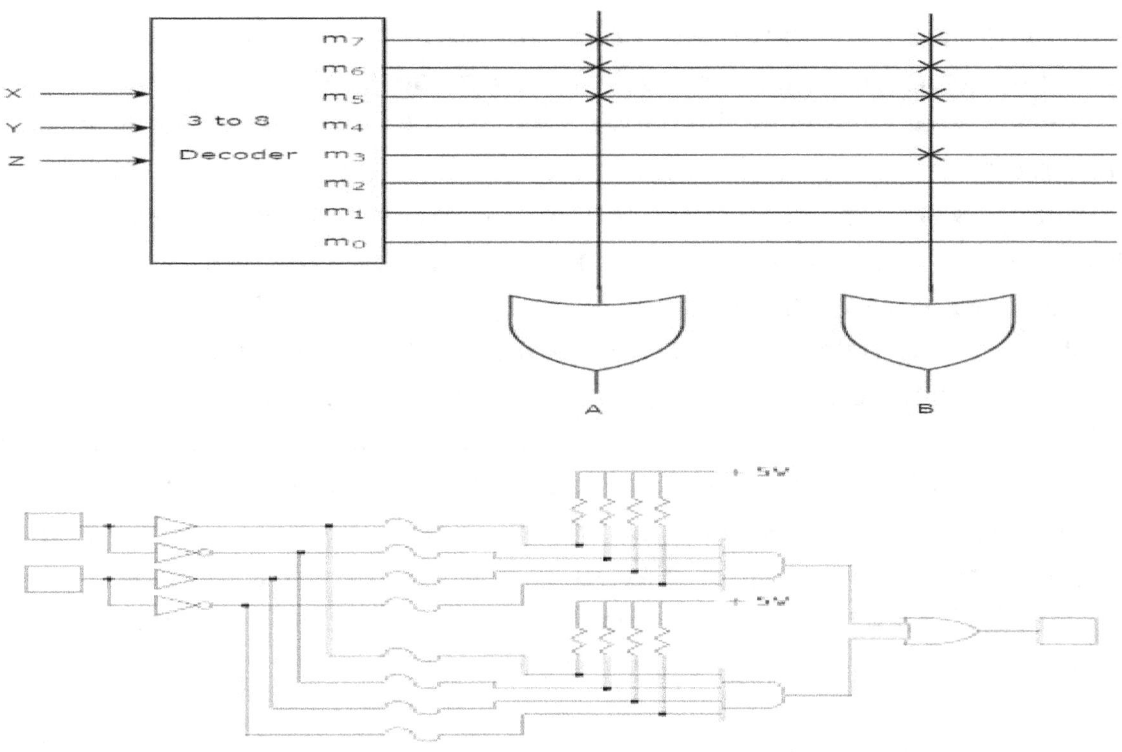

CHAPTER 14

MEMORY DEVICE

The digital processing having storage facility called memory. Memory is of two kind namely semiconductor memory and magnetic memory.

Types of semi-conductor memory

RAM (Random Access Memory)

ROM (Read Only Memory)

14.1 RAM (Random Access Memory)

The simple view of RAM is that it is made up of registers that are made up of flip-flops (or memory elements). The number of flip-flops in a 'memory register' determine the size of the memory word.

14.2 STATIC RAM:

A memory capable of storing data indefinitely, provided there is no loss of power is called static memory. SRAM cell consists of a latch therefore the cell data is kept as long as the power is turned ON and re-fresh operation is not required. SRAM is mainly used for the cache memory in microprocessors, mainframe computer and memory in hand held devices due to high speed and low power conjunction. The data storage cell 1 bit memory cell in static RAM arrays consists of a simple latch circuit with two stable operating points (states). Depending on the present state of the two-inverter latch circuit, data being held in the memory cell will be interpreted either logic 0 or logic 1 . For accessing the data contained in the memory cell via bit line, at least one switch is needle that is controlled by corresponding word line; row address selection signal. Normally, two complementary access switches consisting of NMOS pass transistors are implemented to connect 2 bit SRAM cell to the complementary bit lines (columns). Various configuration of static RAM cell are shown;

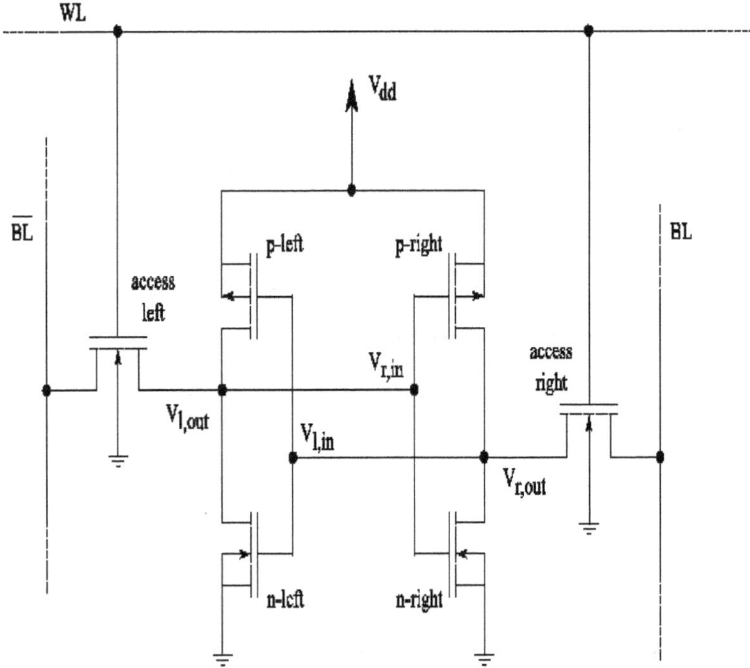

14.3 DYNAMIC RAMS:

Dynamic RAMs are noted for high capacity, moderate access time and low power consumption. Normally their memory cell are basically charge storage capacitor with driver transistor. Presence or absence of charge in a

interpreted by line of logic 1 or logic 0. Dynamic RAMs require periodic charge refreshing to maintain storage of data. Organization of DRAM is also similar to the static RAM.

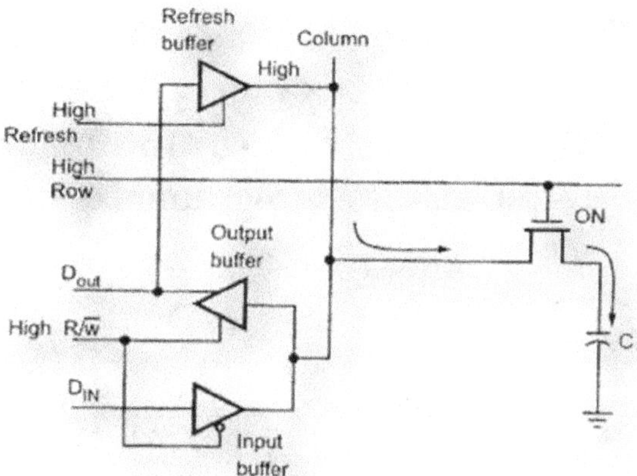

14.4 READ ONLY MEMORY (ROM)

ROM is essentially a memory (or storage) device in which a fixed set of binary information is stored. Once a pattern is established for a ROM, it remains fixed even when power is turned off and turned on again i.e. this is a nonvolatile memory. The concept of an ROM is extremely simple, user supplies address and ROM provides data output of the word prewritten at the address. ROM are internally implemented using diodes, bipolar transistors.

14.5 EEPROM:

These are user programmable and electrically erasable read only memory. Such devices need not be taken out and exposed to UV light. Single bit or entire bytes can be erased instead of erasing the entire chip. The EEPROM takes advantage of same floating gate structure as EPROM. It adds the feature of electrical era's ability through the addition of a thin oxide region above the drain of the MOSFET's gate and drain a charge can be induced onto the floating gate, where it will remain even when power is removed. Reversal of the same voltage causes a removal of trapped charges from the floating gate and erasing of an EEPROM can usually be done in circuit. A major advantage offered by EEPROMs over EPROMs is the ability to electricity erase and reprogram individual words in the memory array.

Another advantage is that a complete EEPROM can be erased in about 10 ms versus almost 30 minutes for an EPROM in external UV light.

14.6 Write two important differences between EPROM and EEPROM

A major advantage of EEPROM over EPROM is the ability to electrically erase and reprogram individual words in the memory array. Another advantage is that a complete EEPROM can be in 10ms (in circuit) 30 minutes for EPROM in external. An EEPROM can also be programmed more rapidly.

14.7. DESIGN OF A FULL ADDER BY PROM

A	B	C	SUM	CARRY
0	0	0	0	0
0	0	1	1	0
0	1	0	1	0
0	1	1	0	1
1	0	0	1	0
1	0	1	0	1
1	1	0	0	1
1	1	1	1	1

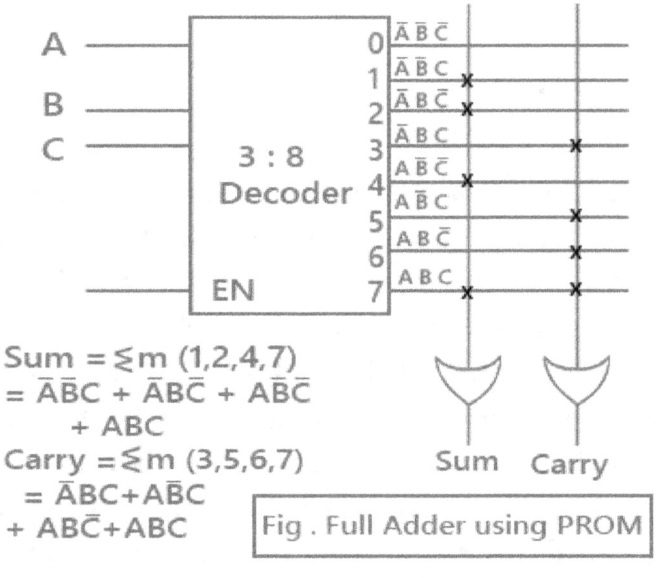

Sum $= \Sigma m\,(1,2,4,7)$
$= \bar{A}\bar{B}C + \bar{A}B\bar{C} + A\bar{B}\bar{C} + ABC$

Carry $= \Sigma m\,(3,5,6,7)$
$= \bar{A}BC + A\bar{B}C + AB\bar{C} + ABC$

Fig . Full Adder using PROM

CHAPTER 15

A/D AND D/A CONVERTER

15.1 WHAT IS A/D AND D/A CONVERTER IN DIGITAL LOGIC DESIGN:

15.1.1 DIGITAL TO ANALOG CONVERTER:

A Digital to Analog Converter (DAC) converts a digital input signal into an analog output signal. The digital signal is represented with a binary code, which is a combination of bits 0 and 1. This chapter deals with Digital to Analog Converters in detail.

15.1.2 TYPES OF DIGITAL TO ANALOG CONVERTER:

a. Weighted Resistor DAC

A weighted resistor DAC produces an analog output, which is almost equal to the digital (binary) input by using binary weighted resistors in the inverting adder circuit. In short, a binary weighted resistor DAC is called as weighted resistor DAC.

The circuit diagram of a 3-bit binary weighted resistor DAC is shown in the following figure –

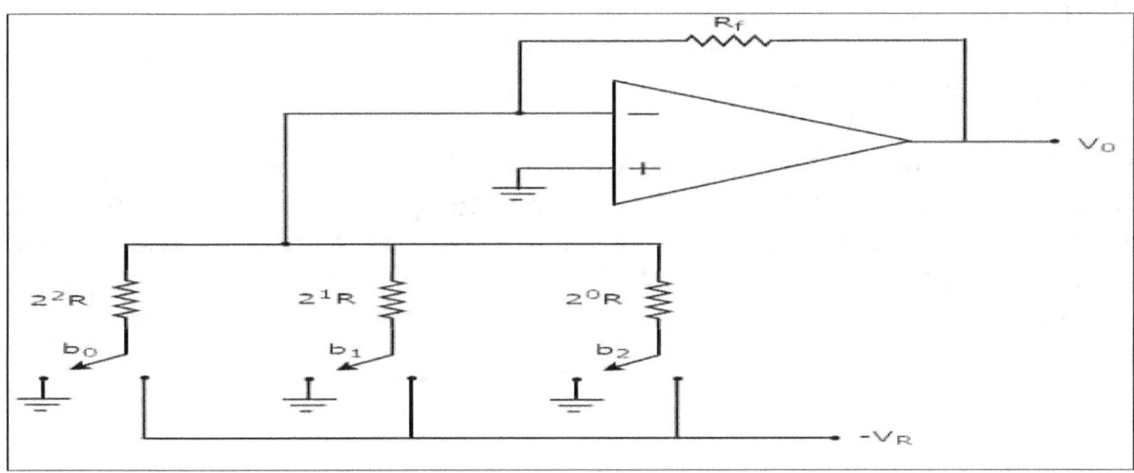

Recall that the bits of a binary number can have only one of the two values. i.e., either 0 or 1. Let the 3-bit binary input is $b_2b_1b_0b_2b_1b_0$. Here, the bits b_2b_2 and b_0b_0 denote the Most Significant Bit (MSB) and Least Significant Bit (LSB) respectively.

The digital switches shown in the above figure will be connected to ground, when the corresponding input bits are equal to '0'. Similarly, the digital switches shown in the above figure will be connected to the negative reference voltage, $-V_R$ $-VR$ when the corresponding input bits are equal to '1'.

In the above circuit, the non-inverting input terminal of an op-amp is connected to ground. That means zero volts is applied at the non-inverting input terminal of op-amp.

According to the virtual short concept, the voltage at the inverting input terminal of opamp is same as that of the voltage present at its non-inverting input terminal. So, the voltage at the inverting input terminal's node will be zero volts.

The nodal equation at the inverting input terminal's node is:

$$0+V_R b_2/2_0 R+0+V_R b_1/2_1 R+0+V_R b_0/2_2 R+(0-V_0)/R_f=0$$

$$=>V_0/R_f=V_R b_2/2_0 R+V_R b_1/2_1 R+V_R b_0/2_2 R$$

$$=>V_0=V_R R_f/R\{b_2/2_0+b_1/2_1+b_0/2_2\}$$

Substituting, $R=2R_f$ $R=2Rf$ f in above equation.

$$=>V_0=V_R R_f/2R_f\{b_2/2_0+b_1/2_1+b_0/2_2\}$$

$$=>V_0=V_R/2\{b_2/2_0+b_1/2_1+b_0/2_2\}$$

b. R-2R Ladder DAC

The R-2R Ladder DAC overcomes the disadvantages of a binary weighted resistor DAC. As the name suggests, R-2R Ladder DAC produces an analog output, which is almost equal to the digital (binary) input by using a R-2R ladder network in the inverting adder circuit.

The circuit diagram of a 3-bit R-2R Ladder DAC is shown in the following figure –

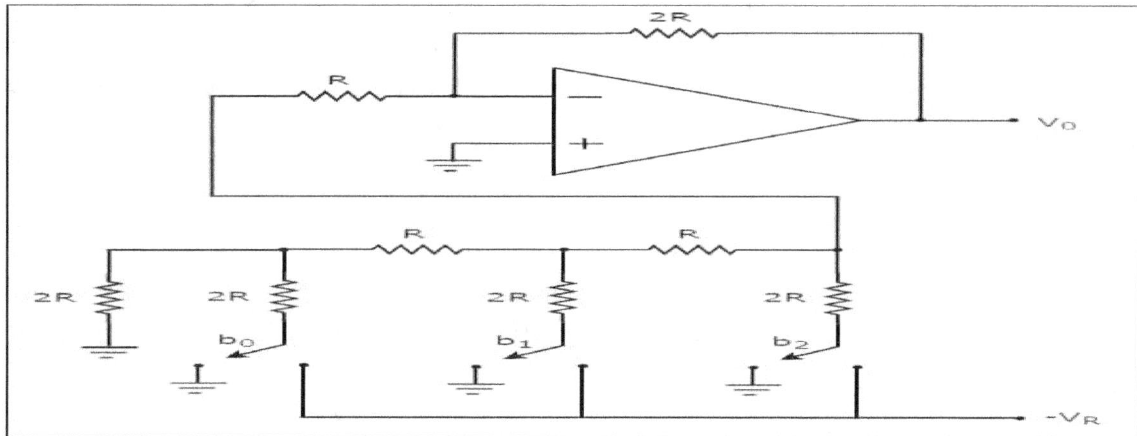

Recall that the bits of a binary number can have only one of the two values. i.e., either 0 or 1. Let the 3-bit binary input **is** $b_2b_1b_0b_2b_1b_0$**. Here, the bits** b_2b_2 **and** b_0b_0 **denote the Most Significant Bit (MSB) and Least Significant Bit (LSB) respectively.**

The digital switches shown in the above figure will be connected to ground, when the corresponding input bits are equal to '0'. Similarly, the digital switches shown in above figure will be connected to the negative reference voltage, $-V_R-V_R$ **when the corresponding input bits are equal to '1'.**

It is difficult to get the generalized output voltage equation of a R-2R Ladder DAC. But, we can find the analog output voltage values of R-2R Ladder DAC for individual binary input combinations easily.

15.1.3 ANALOG TO DIGITAL CONVERTER:

An analog-to-digital converter (ADC) is used to convert an analog signal such as voltage to a digital form so that it can be read and processed by a microcontroller. Most microcontrollers nowadays have built-in ADC converters. It is also possible to connect an external ADC converter to any type of microcontroller. ADC converters are usually 10 or 12 bits, having 1024–4096 quantization levels.
The ADC conversion process must be started by the user program and it may take several hundreds of microseconds for a conversion to complete. ADC converters usually generate interrupts when a conversion is complete so that the user program can read the converted data as quickly as possible. ADC converters are very useful in control and monitoring applications since most sensors in real life (e.g., temperature sensor, pressure sensor, , etc.) produce analog output voltages.

15.1.4 DUAL-SLOPE ADC:

The advantage of dual-slope ADC is in relatively low cost but it has one of the slowest conversion times (typically 10 to 100 ms). Basic operation involves linear charging discharging of a capacitor using constant current. The major advantage of it is in low sensitivity to noise.

15.1.5 FLASH TYPE ADC:

It is the highest speed ADC but it is much more circuiting then other type. Normally a flash type ADC remaining (2^N-1) comparator. 2^N resistors and encoder logic.

15.1.6 SUCCESSIVE APPROXIMATION ADC:

This type of ADC has complex circuiting but it has a much shorter conversion time. Mor-ever it has fixed value of conversion time that is not dependent on analog input value.

i.   **Transfer Characteristics:**

       A typical transfer characteristics of an ADC is displayed below; 3 bit digital code changes from one to the next higher code at a certain discrete value of V_{in}

ii.   **Sampling Frequency:**

       The sampling frequency (min) must be at least double the highest frequency content of the signal.

iii.   **Resolution:**

       The resolution of an ADC depends on the size of the quantum interval of the analog input for which digital code changes from one value to the next.

CHAPTER-16

CONCLUSION

Author has written this book on the looking or observing the common academic syllabus of digital logic system design in electronics technology as per the criteria's of electrical and electronics department. That's why author has displayed common chapters available in digital logic design system so that the students can learn the subjects for the semester purpose only. But this book author has not composed for laboratory purpose; because already author has composed such a book on digital electronics design laboratory available in the market. So, if students want more rectifications in this book then they can consult some other books also on digital electronics also but conceptual formulae's of the problems will remain same as mentioned in the book.

[ANNEXTURE BOOK-2]

DIGITAL COMMUNICATION THEORITICAL HANDBOOK OF GRADUATE ENGINEERING STUDENT

ABSTRACT

The author has already designed an academic book of analog advanced and microwave communication; likewise analog, advanced and microwave communication; likewise analog part of communication is based on continuous periodic and aperiodic domain of signal communication . Now author is concentrating on digital or discrete sequence of data communication. So in this book of digital communication the author has decided analyze and explain several chapters of digital communication engineering for graduate electronics engineering students. Now this is a short handbook based on very common chapters of digital communication where author has used limited mat-lab codes to justify some typical methodologies of digital communication technology; students may use different mat-lab codes but theoretical discussion is important for everyone.

INDEX

SL NO	NAME OF THE CHAPTER	PAGE NO
1	INTRODUCTION	65
2	WHAT IS TIME DIVISION MULTIPLEXING	65
3	EXPLAIN TIME DIVISION MULTIPLEXING	65-67
4	WHAT IS FREQUENCY DIVISION MULTIPLEXING	67
5	EXPLAIN FRQUENCY DIVISION MULTIPLEXING	68
6	COMPARION BETWEEN TDM AND FDM	69
7	PRINCIPLE OF AMPLITUDE SHIFT KEYING	69-71
8	MATLAB CODE OF AMPLITUDE SHIFT KEYING	72
9	PRINCIPLE OF FREQUENCY SHIFT KEYING	73-75
10	MATLAB CODE OF FREQUENCY SHIFT KEYING	76-78
11	PRINCIPLE OF PHASE SHIFT KEYING	78-80
12	MATLAB CODE OF PHASE SHIFT KEYING	81-82
13	SHORT DISCUSSION ON QPSK, QAM	83-86
14	MATLAB CODE OF QAM, QPSK	87-89
15	BASIC DISCUSSION OF INFORMATION THEORY	90-95
16	QANTISATION THERORY AND DELTA MODULTATION TECHNIQUE	96-102
17	CONCLUSION	102

CHAPTER-1

INTRODUCTION

In this short hand book the author has already described in abstract section what he is going to discuss about the fundamentals of book on digital communication. Mainly the author is focusing on digital modulation technology and technology based on information theory analysis. One set of mat-lab programming has been explained for ASK, PSK and FSK modulation technique and mostly common chapters have been discussed in this book only.

CHAPTER-2

WHAT IS TIME DIVISION MULTIPLEXING

This happens when the data transmission rate of media is greater than that of the source, and each signal is allotted a definite amount of time. These slots are so small that all transmissions appear to be parallel. In frequency division multiplexing all the signals operate at the same time with different frequencies, but in time-division multiplexing, all the signals operate with the same frequency at different times.

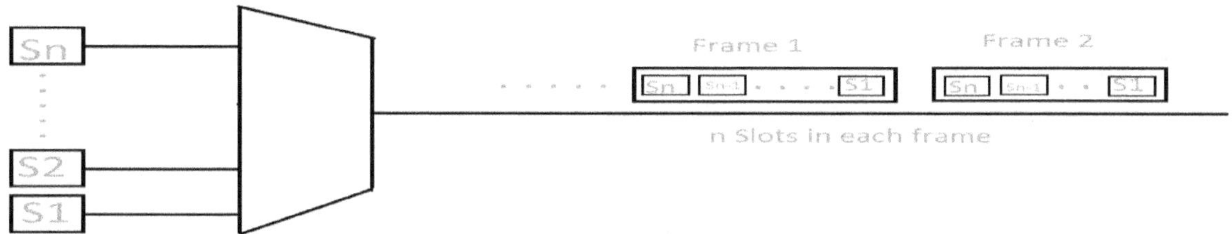

CHAPTER-3

EXPLAIN WHAT IS TIME DIVISION MULTIPLEXING

Time division multiplexing of the following types:

3.1. Synchronous TDM:

The time slots are pre-assigned and fixed. This slot is even given if the source is not ready with data at this time. In this case, the slot is transmitted empty. It is used for multiplexing digitized voice streams.

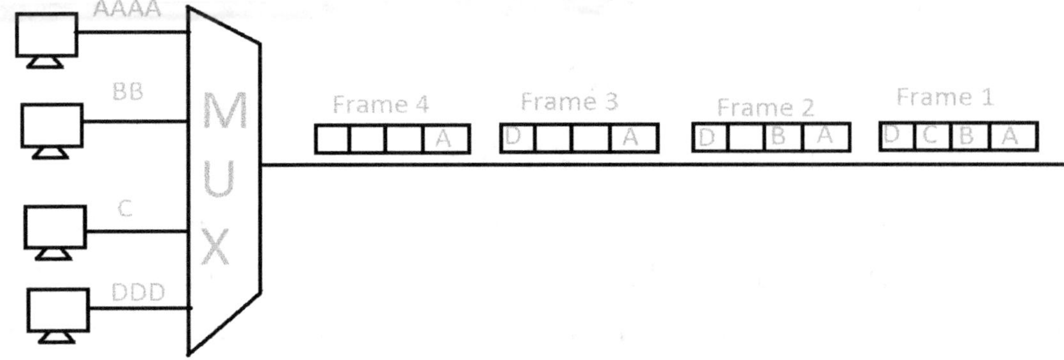

3.2 Asynchronous (or statistical) TDM:

The slots are allocated dynamically depending on the speed of the source or their ready state. It dynamically allocates the time slots according to different input channels' needs, thus saving the channel capacity.

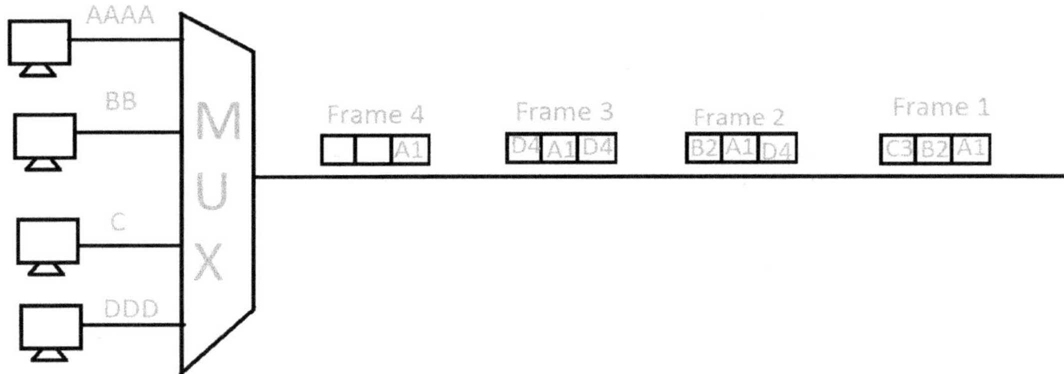

3.3 Advantages of Time Division Multiplexing (TDM):

High Capacity: TDM can support a large number of signals over a single communication channel, making it ideal for applications where many signals need to be transmitted.
Simple Implementation: TDM is a relatively simple technique that is easy to implement, making it a cost-effective solution for many applications.
Precise Time Synchronization: TDM requires precise time synchronization between the transmitting and receiving devices, which can help ensure accurate transmission of signals.

3.4 Disadvantages of Time Division Multiplexing (TDM):

Inefficient Use of Bandwidth: TDM may not make optimal use of available bandwidth, as time slots may be left unused if there are no signals to transmit during a particular time slot. High Implementation Cost: TDM requires sophisticated hardware or software to ensure precise time synchronization between the transmitting and receiving devices, making it more expensive to implement than FDM. Vulnerable to Timing Jitter: TDM can be vulnerable to timing jitter, which can occur when the timing of the transmitting and receiving devices drifts out of sync, leading to errors in the transmission of signals.

CHAPTER-4

WHAT IS FREQUENCY DIVISION MULTIPLEXING

In this, a number of signals are transmitted at the same time, and each source transfers its signals in the allotted frequency range. There is a suitable frequency gap between the 2 adjacent signals to avoid overlapping. Since the signals are transmitted in the allotted frequencies so this decreases the probability of collision. The frequency spectrum is divided into several logical channels, in which every user feels that they possess a particular bandwidth. A number of signals are sent simultaneously at the same time allocating separate frequency bands or channels to each signal. It is used in radio and TV transmission. Therefore to avoid interference between two successive channels Guard bands are used.

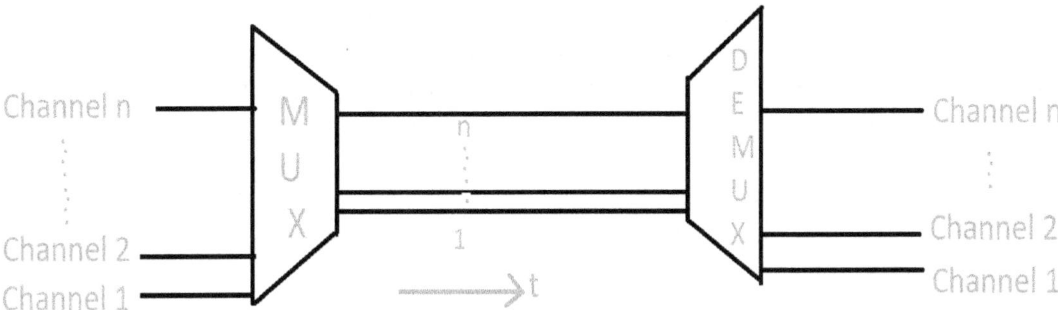

CHAPTER-5

EXPLAIN WHAT IS FREQUENCY DIVISION MULTIPLEXING

5.1 Advantages of Frequency Division Multiplexing (FDM):

Efficient Use of Bandwidth: FDM allows multiple signals to be transmitted over a single communication channel, which can lead to more efficient use of available bandwidth. No Time Synchronization Required: FDM does not require precise time synchronization between the transmitting and receiving devices, making it easier to implement. Low Implementation Cost: FDM is a relatively simple technique that does not require sophisticated hardware or software, making it less expensive to implement.

5.2 Disadvantages of Frequency Division Multiplexing (FDM):

Limited Capacity: FDM is limited in terms of the number of signals that can be transmitted over a single communication channel, which can be a disadvantage in applications where a large number of signals need to be transmitted. Interference: FDM can be susceptible to interference from other signals transmitted on nearby frequencies, which can degrade the quality of the transmitted signals. Difficulty in Assigning Frequencies: FDM requires careful assignment of frequencies to different signals to avoid interference, which can be a complex and time-consuming process.

5.3 Application of FDM:

1. In the first generation of mobile phones, FDM was used.
2. The use of FDM in television broadcasting
3. FDM is used to broadcast FM and AM radio frequencies

CHAPTER-6

COMPARION BETWEEN TDM AND FDM

Difference between TDM and FDM

The following table highlights the major differences between TDM and FDM.

Key	TDM	FDM
Definition	TDM stands for Time Division Multiplexing.	FDM stands for Frequency Division Multiplexing.
Signal	TDM works well with both analog as well as digital signals.	FDM works only with analog signal.
Conflict	TDM has low conflict.	FDM has high conflict.
Wiring	Wiring or Chip of TDM is simpler.	Wiring or Chip of FDM is complex.
Efficiency	TDM is efficient	FDM is quiet inefficient.
Sharing	Time is shared in TDM.	Frequency is shared in FDM.
Required Input	Synchronization pulse is mandatory in TDM.	Synchronization pulse is not mandatory.

CHAPTER-7

PRINCIPLE OF AMPLITUDE SHIFT KEYING

Let a sinusoidal carrier signal= $A * \cos(2*pi*f_c*t)$

ASK signal representation=

$s(t) = A * \cos(2*pi*f_c*t)$ for symbol 1

     $= 0$ for symbol 0

Peak amplitude $A = \sqrt{2*E/T}$

7.1 GENERATION OF ASK SIGNAL:

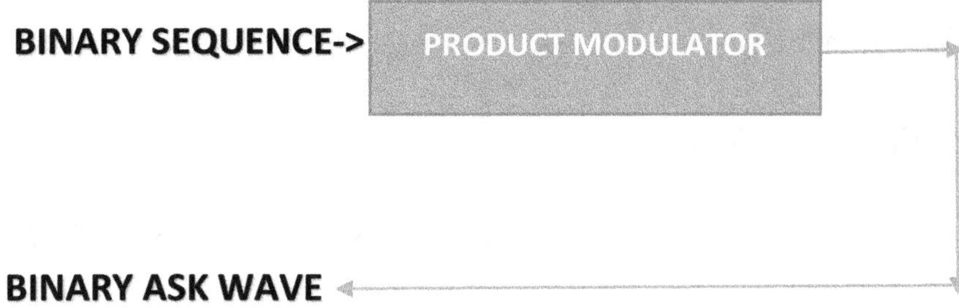

7.2 DEMODULATION OF ASK

7.2.1 COHERENT DETECTION:

In coherent detection we need a carrier signal for detection and synchronous with Binary ASK wave; there is an integrator and a decision making device connected with threshold ; if result of integrator exceeds threshold decision will be 1.

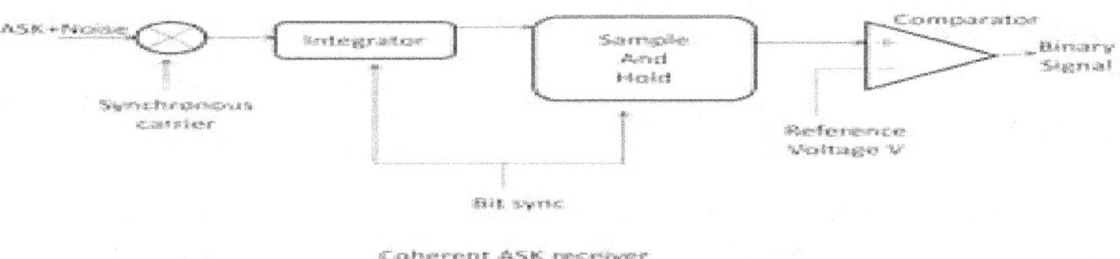

7.2.2 NON COHERENT DETECTION:

In non-coherent detection no carrier signal is there or present. Instead of integrator there is an envelop detector combination of rectifier and lpf.

7.2.3 Advantages of ASK

The wave generated is quite simple to detect and generate

7.2.4 Disadvantages of ASK

a. It has very poor bandwidth efficiency
b. The generated signal is extremely susceptible to external factors like noise.
c. It is not fit for high bit rate data transmission.

7.2.5 ASK Applications

Some of the important applications of ASK has been mentioned below:

a. Low-frequency RF applications
b. Industrial networks devices
c. Tire pressuring monitoring systems

d. Wireless base stations

7.2.6 Input-Output bit sequence diagram of ASK

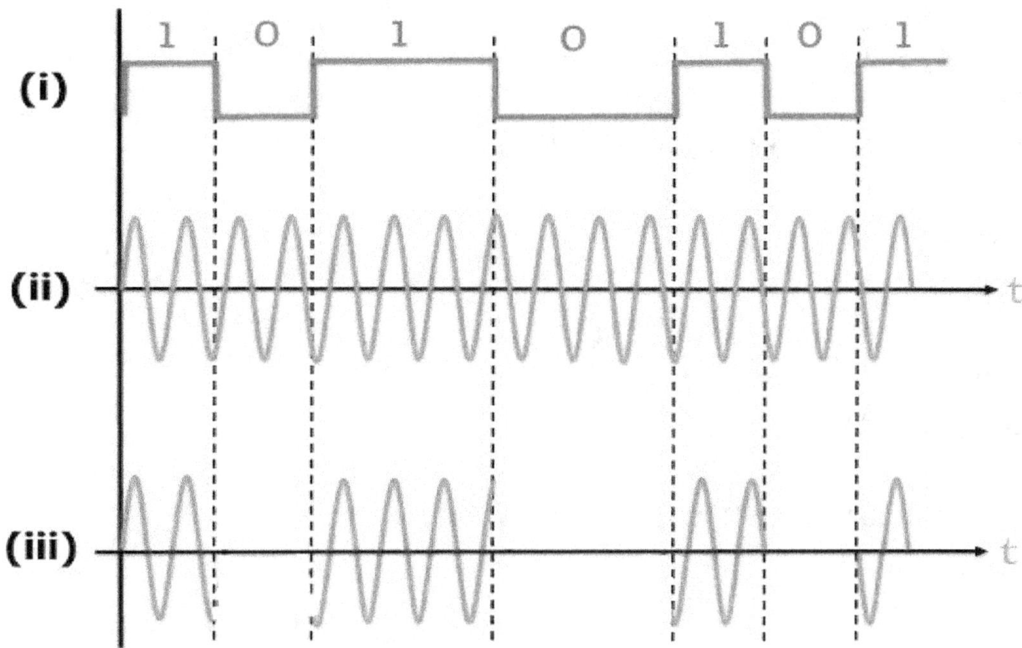

(i) = Digital bit sequence
(ii) = Carrier wave
(iii) = ASK modulated wave

CHAPTER-8
MATLAB CODE OF AMPLITUDE SHIFT KEYING

8.1 MATLAB CODES:

```
b=input('Enter the bit stream\n');%b=[0 1 0 1 1 1 0];
Enter the bit stream
[0 1 0 1 1 1 0]
n=length(b);
t=0:.01:n;
x=1:1:(n+1)*100;
for i=1:n
for j=1:1:i+1
bw(x(i*100:(i+1)*100))=b(i);
end
end
 bw=bw(100:end);
 sint=sin(2*pi*t);
 st=bw.*sint;
 subplot(3,1,1)
 plot(t,bw)
 title("original bit sequence");
 grid on;
 subplot(3,1,2)
 plot(t,sint)
 title("modulating signal");
 grid on;
 subplot(3,1,3)
 plot(t,st)
 title("modulated ASK signal");
 grid on;
```

8.2 OUTPUT FIGURE:

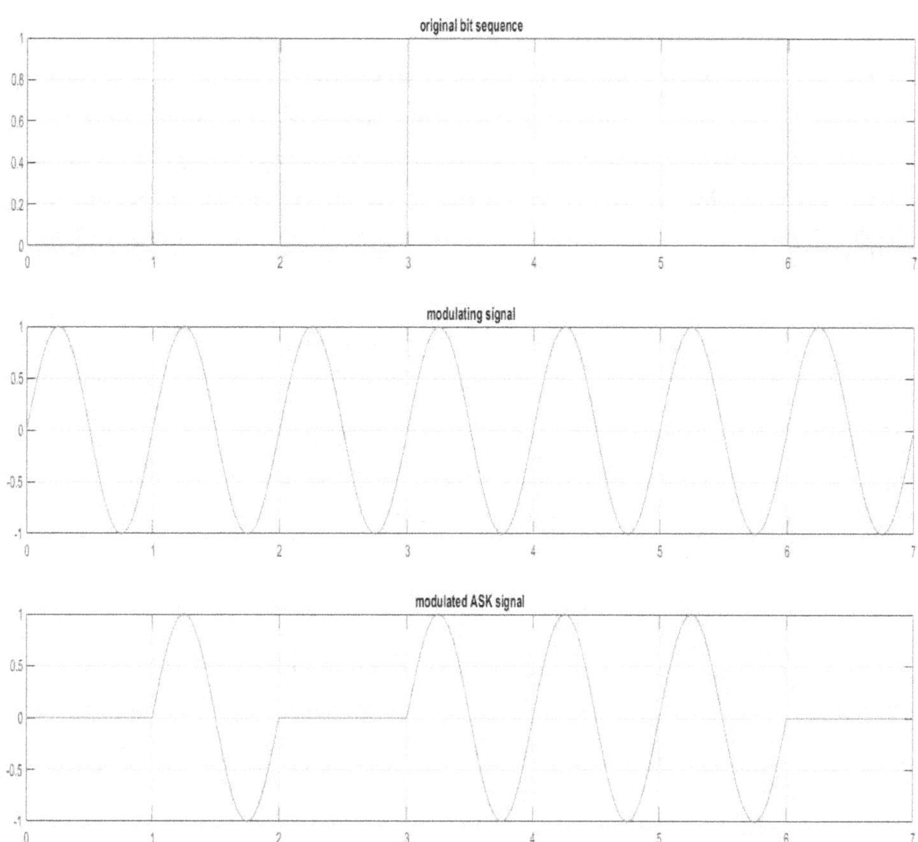

CHAPTER-9

PRINCIPLE OF FREQUENCY SHIFT KEYING

Let the sinusoidal carrier =x(t)=A*cos(2*pi*f_c*t)

S(t)=sqrt(2P)*cos 2*pi*(f_c+del(f))t for symbol 1

   = sqrt(2P)*cos 2*pi*(f_c-del(f))t for symbol 0

S(t)=sqrt(P*t_b)*sqrt(2/T_b)*cos(2*pi*f_1*t) for symbol 1

   = sqrt(P*t_b)*sqrt(2/T_b)*cos(2*pi*f_2*t) for symbol 0

9.1 Generation of FSK signal

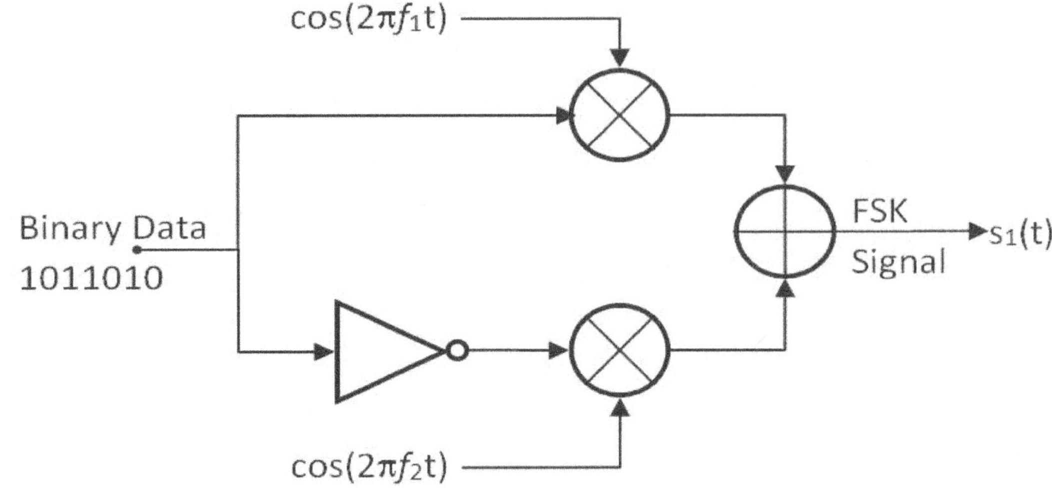

9.2 DEMODULATION OF FSK SIGNAL:

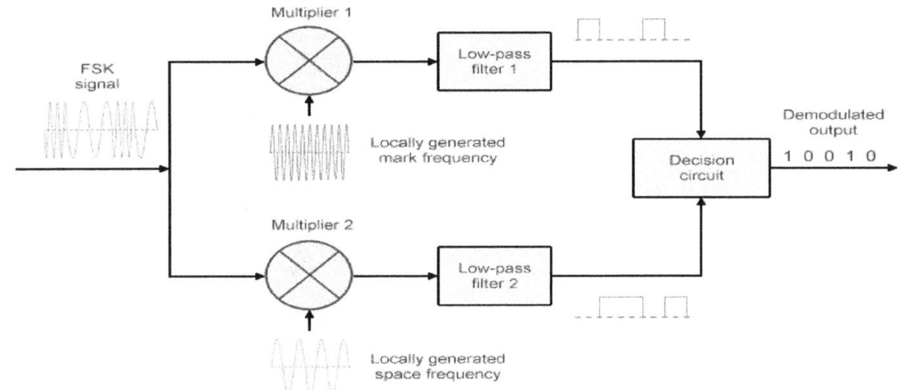

In coherent detection two synchronous carrier signals are required multiplied by two multiplier. There will be a comparison between two integrators outputs here low pass filters we have used as integrator.

9.3 NON COHERENT DETECTION OF FSK

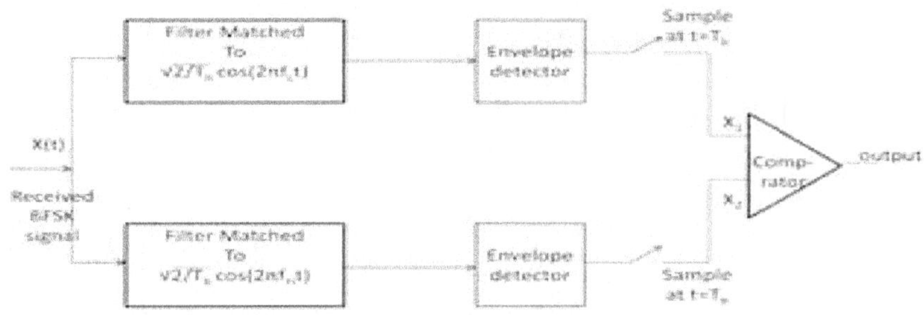

No carrier signal is required for synchronisation with the modulated FSK wave.

9.4 BIT DIAGRAM OF FSK SIGNALS:

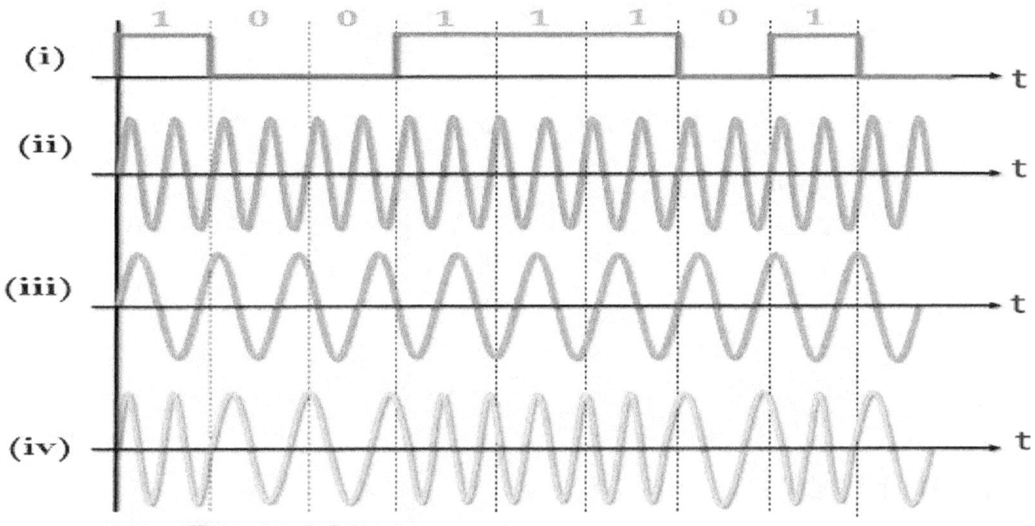

CHAPTER-10
MATLAB CODE OF FREQUENCY SHIFT KEYING

10.1 MATLAB CODE:

```matlab
b=input('enter the bit stream\n');%b=[0 1 0 1 1 1 0];

enter the bit stream

[0 1 0 1 1 1 0]

n=length(b);

t=0:.01:n;

x=1:1:(n+1)*100;

for i=1:n

if(b(i)==0)

b_p(i)=-1;

else

b_p(i)=1;

end

for j=i:.1:i+1

bw(x(i*100:(i+1)*100))=b_p(i);

end

end

bw=bw(100:end);

w0=2*(2*pi*t);

W=1*(2*pi*t);

sinHt=sin(w0+W);
```

```
sinLt=sin(w0-W);

st=sin(w0+(bw).*W);

subplot(4,1,1)

plot(t,bw)

title(" input bit sequence");

grid on;

subplot(4,1,2)

plot(t,sinHt)

title(" modulating signal");

grid on;

subplot(4,1,3)

plot(t,sinLt)

title("modulated FSK signal")

grid on;
```

10.2 OUTPUT FIGURE:

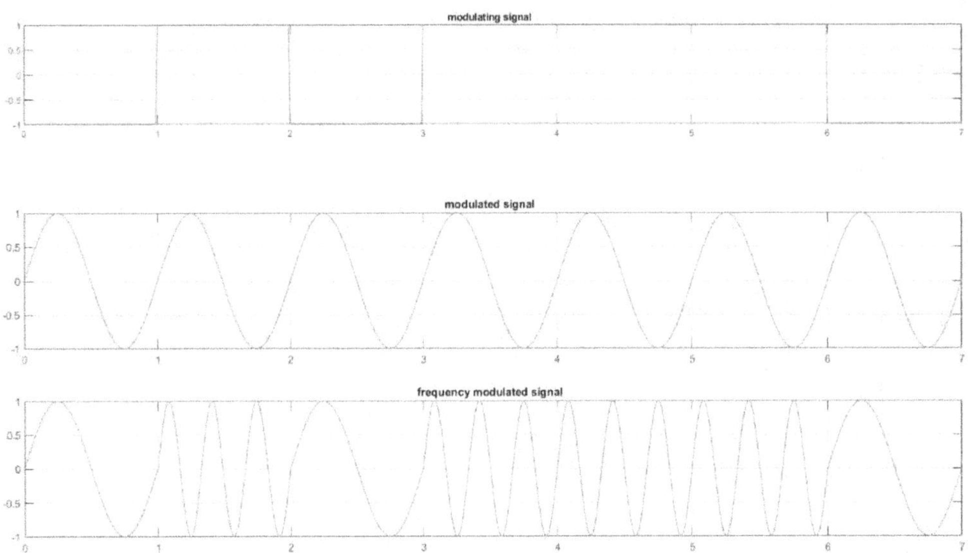

CHAPTER-11

PRINCIPLE OF PHASE SHIFT KEYING

Let the sinusoidal carrier is x(t)=A*cos(2*pi*f$_c$*t)

BPSK signals

x(t)=sqrt(2*P)*cos(2*pi*f$_c$*t)

=sqrt(2P)* cos(2*pi*f$_c$*t+180·)

=-sqrt(2P)*cos(2*pi*f$_c$*t)

11.1 Generation of PSK

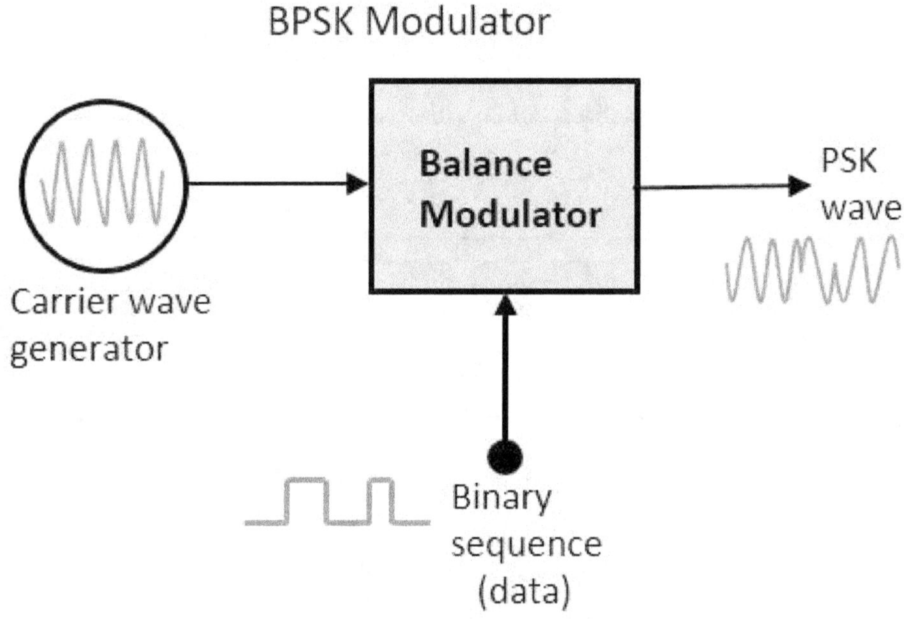

11.2 Demodulation of PSK:

In coherent detection the synchronization problem can be recovered by the use of DPSK technique which is non coherent detection technique.

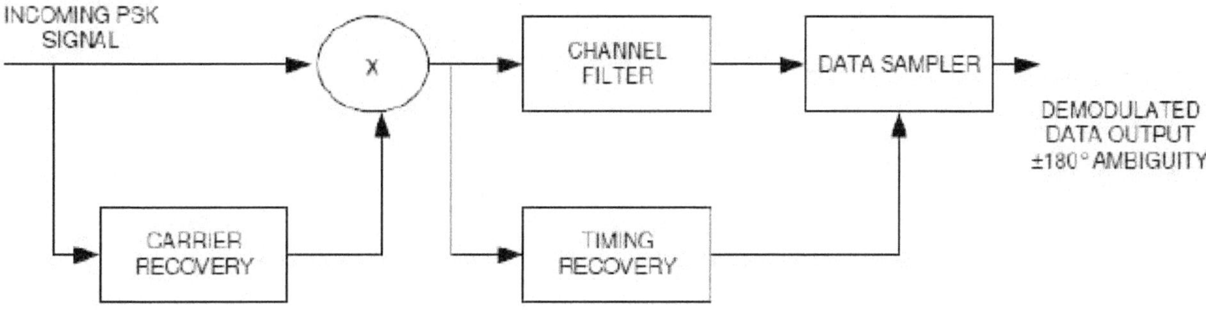

11.3 Input bit sequence diagram of PSK:

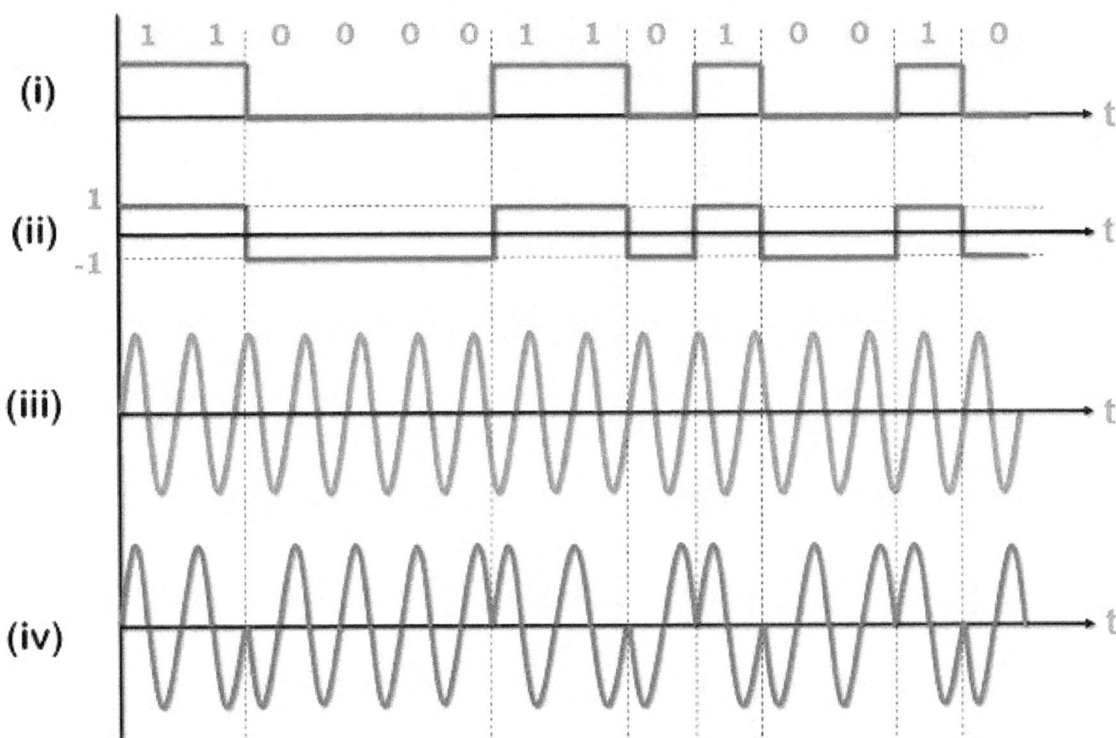

(i)   Binary data sequence
(ii) Bipolar NRZ sequence
(iii) Carrier wave
(iv) BPSK waveform

CHAPTER-12

MATLAB CODE OF PHASE SHIFT KEYING MODULATION

12.1 MATLAB CODE:

```
b=input('enter the bit stream\n');%b=[0 1 0 1 1 1 0];

enter the bit stream

[0 1 0 1 1 1 0]

n=length(b);

t=0:.01:n;

x=1:1:(n+1)*100;

for i=1:n

if(b(i)==0)

b_p(i)=-1;

else

b_p(i)=1;

end

for j=i:.1:i+1

bw(x(i*100:(i+1)*100))=b_p(i);

end

end

bw=bw(100:end);

sint=sin(2*pi*t);

st=bw.*sint;

subplot(3,1,1)

plot(t,bw)
```

```
grid on;

title('modulating signal');

subplot(3,1,2)

plot(t,sint)

grid on;

title('modulated signal');

subplot(3,1,3)

plot(t,st)

grid on;

title('phase shift modulated signal');
```

12.2 OUTPUT FIGURE:

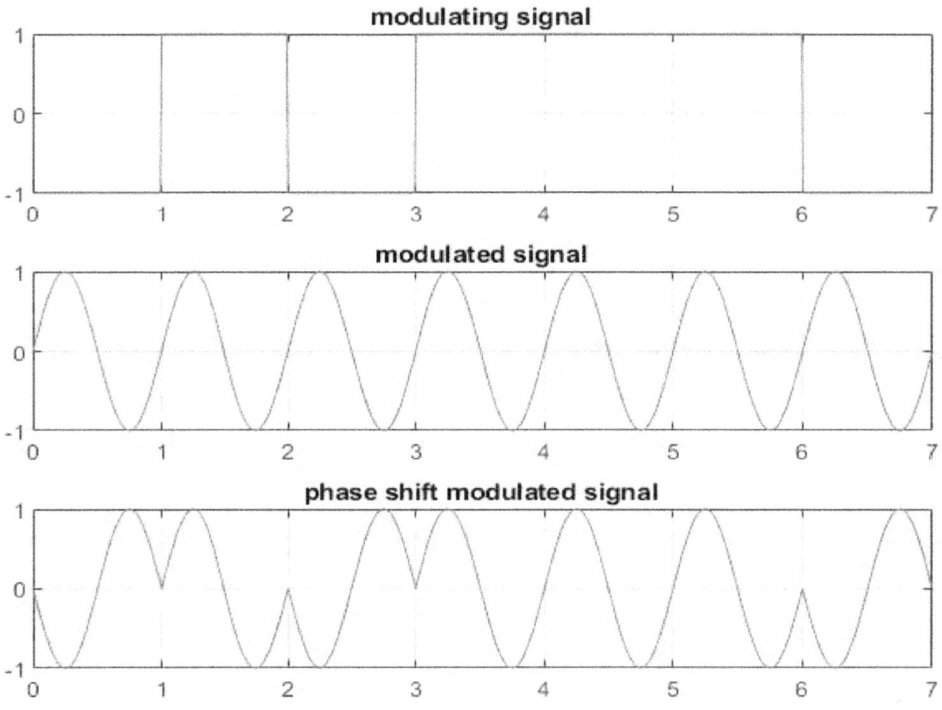

CHAPTER-13

SHORT DISCUSSION ON QPSK, QAM

13.1 WHAT IS QUADRATURE PHASE SHIFT KEYING

QPSK, sometimes known as 4-PSK or 4-QAM , is a digital modulation technique in which two successive bits in the data sequence are grouped together to reduce the bit rate or signaling rate and thus reducing the bandwidth bandwidth of the channel. In BPSK owing to presence of only two symbols, the phase shift occurs in two levels only. In case of QPSK, the combination of two bits from four distinct symbols. Thus, when the symbol , the phase of the carrier changes by 45 degree (pi/4 radians). The QPSK signal is given by;

$S_n(t)=sqrt(2p)*cos(2*pi*f_c*t+(2*n-1)*pi/4]$

Which yields the four phases pi/4, 3*pi/4, 5*pi/4, 7*pi/4 as needed. The QPSK transmits twice the data rate in a given bandwidth as compared to BPSK at the bit error rate. QPSK finds extensive applications in CDMA system, cable modem, video conferencing, satellite communication etc.

n	Input successive bits		symbols	Phase shift in carrier
1	1	0	S_1	pi/4
2	0	0	S_2	3*pi/4
3	0	1	S_3	5*pi/4
4	1	1	S_4	7*pi/4

13.3 Mathematical Representation

Let the binary data sequence b(t) which is broken down to odd and even numbered bit sequence by a de-multiplexer as $b_e(t)$ and $b_o(t)$ respectively. Let the two quadrature carrier signals be represented as $sqrt(P_S)*cos(2*pi*f_c*t)$ and $sqrt(P_S)*sin(2*pi*f_c*t)$. Thus the modulated signals obtained after multiplying the odd and even numbered bit sequence with quadrature carrier signals be represented by

$S_0(t)=b_o(t)*sqrt(P_S)* cos(2*pi*f_c*t)$

$S_e(t) = b_e(t) * sqrt(P_S) * \sin(2*pi*f_c*t)$

Hence QPSK signal is given by

$s(t) = s_e(t) + s_0(t) = b_0(t) * sqrt(P_S) * \cos(2*pi*f_c*t) + b_e(t) * sqrt(P_S) * \sin(2*pi*f_c*t)$

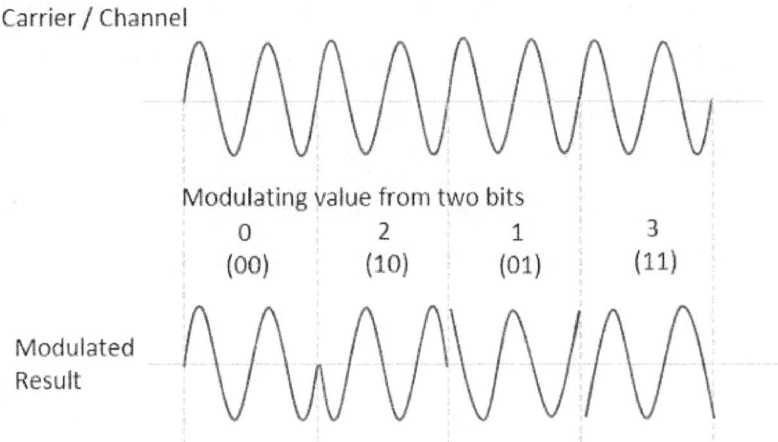

13.2 GENERATION OF QPSK SIGNAL:

The block diagram depicting generation of QPSK signal as displayed in the figure; here the binary data sequence in bipolar NRZ form is fed to a de-multiplexer circuit. The de-multiplexer divides the incoming bit stream into odd and even numbered bit sequence where each sequence has a symbol duration of $2*T_b$. Every symbol here is of two bits. The de-multiplexer output is fed to two product modulators (balanced modulators). The other input to the two respective modulators are two quadrature carrier signals sqrt(P_S)* cos(2*pi*f_c*t) and sqrt(P_S)* sin(2*pi*f_c*t) respectively. The modulator outputs are fed to an adder circuit which produces at its output a QPSK signal.

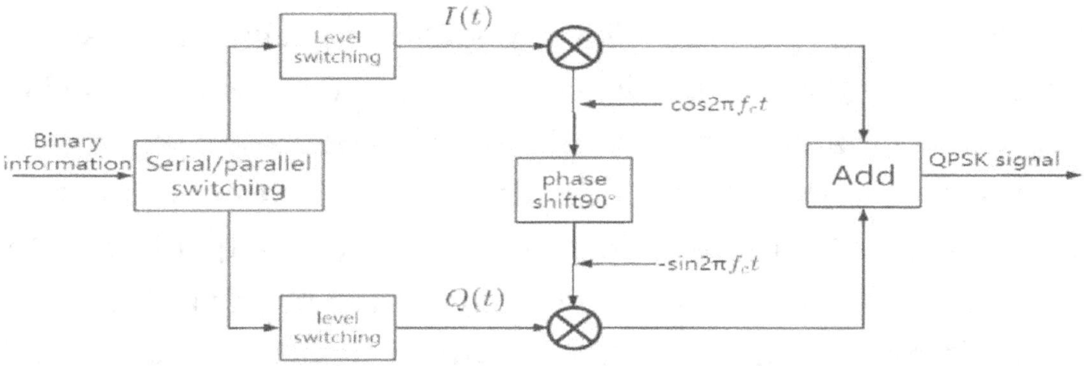

13.3 DEMODULATION OF QPSK SIGNAL:

The synchronous detection scheme of QPSK signal has been displayed in the below mentioned figure; the two coherent quadrature carriers are recovered from the incoming QPSK wave and are applied to the two synchronous demodulators and co-rrelators each comprising of multiplier and an integrator. The multiplier multiplies the incoming QPSK signal with respective carrier signal and its output is fed to the integrator. The integrator integrates over two bit intervals and the respective integrators output are ultimately fed to a multiplexer circuit. The multiplexer combines the odd and even bit sequences and produces at its output the complete binary bit sequence.

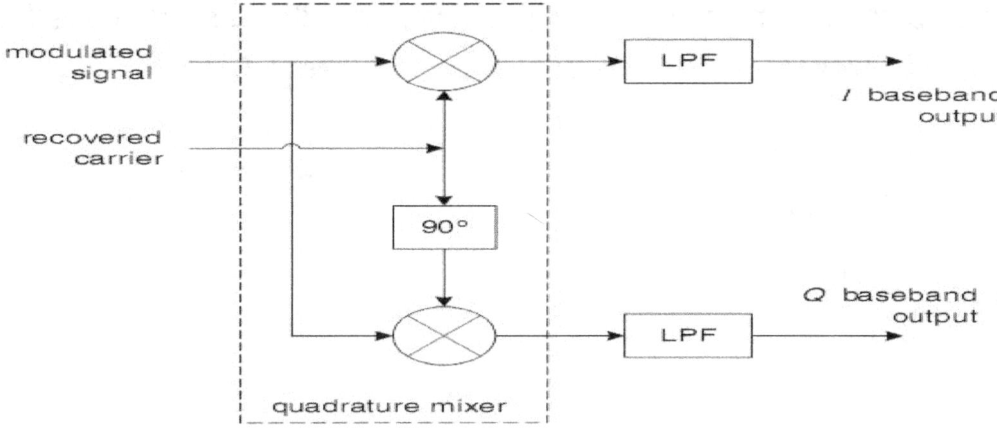

13.4 QUADRATURE AMPLITUDE MODULATION TECHNIQUES:

QAM is both an analog and a digital modulation technique in which two message signals or two digital streams are transmitted using ASK digital modulator scheme or AM analog modulation scheme. In this technique, two different signals are transmitted using two carriers which are of the same frequency but at phase quadrature to each other. By this techniques the transmission bandwidth is one-half the bandwidth required if the individual signals are modulated using different carriers. If the two baseband signals to the transmitted are $m_1(t)$ and $m_2(t)$, the corresponding DSB modulated signals are $m_1(t)*cos(w_ct)$ (in phase) and $m_2(t)*sin(w_ct)$ [quadrature] . The I and Q signals fed to the adder produces QAM signal as its output which is expressed as

$$s(t)= m_1(t)*cos(w_ct)+ m_2(t)*sin(w_ct)$$

Both modulated signals occupy the same band, yet two baseband signals can be separated at the receiver by synchronous detection using two local in phase quadrature as displayed, this can be represented as:

$$X_1(t)= 2*[m_1(t)*cos(w_c*t)+m_2(t)*sin(w_c*t)]*cos(w_c*t)$$

$$=m_1(t)+m_1(t)*cos(2*w_c*t)+m_2(t)*sin(2*w_c*t)$$

The last two terms are of high frequency and will be suppressed by the low pass filter yirelding the desired output $m_1(t)$.

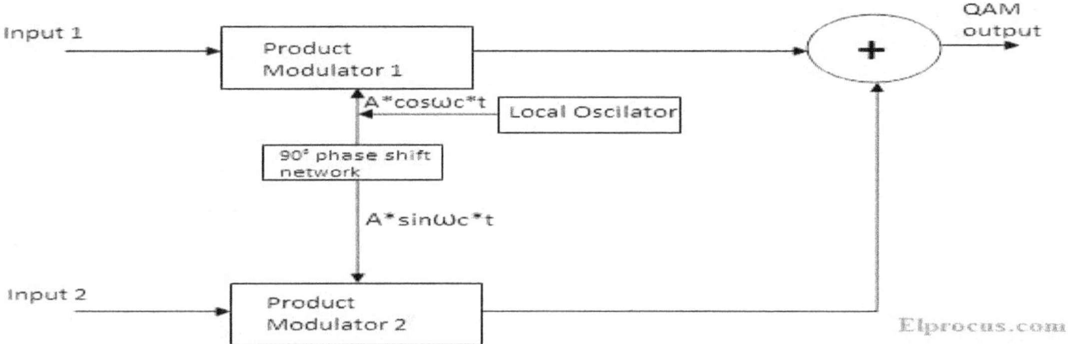

CHAPTER-14

MATLAB CODE OF QPSK MODULATOR AND DEMODULATOR, QAM

14.1 MATLAB CODE OF QPSK

mod = comm.QPSKModulator;

refC = constellation(mod)

refC =

  0.7071 + 0.7071i

 -0.7071 + 0.7071i

 -0.7071 - 0.7071i

  0.7071 - 0.7071i

constellation(mod)

demod = comm.QPSKDemodulator(0);

constellation(demod)

14.2 OUTPUT DIAGRAM OF QPSK MODULATOR AND DEMODULATOR:

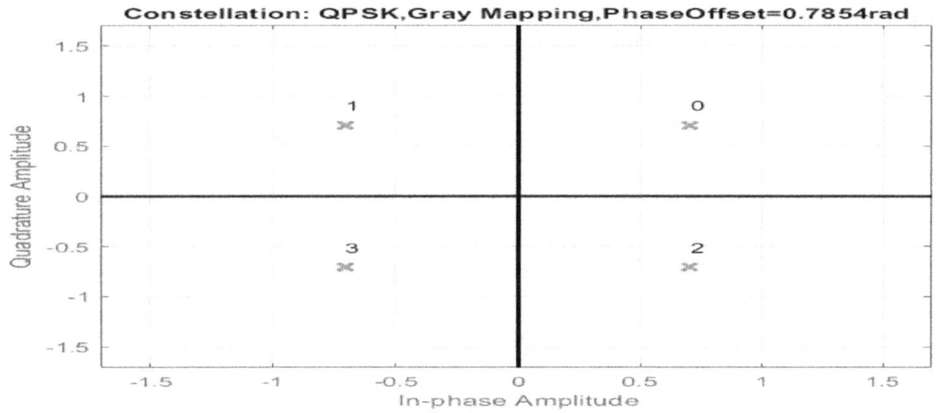

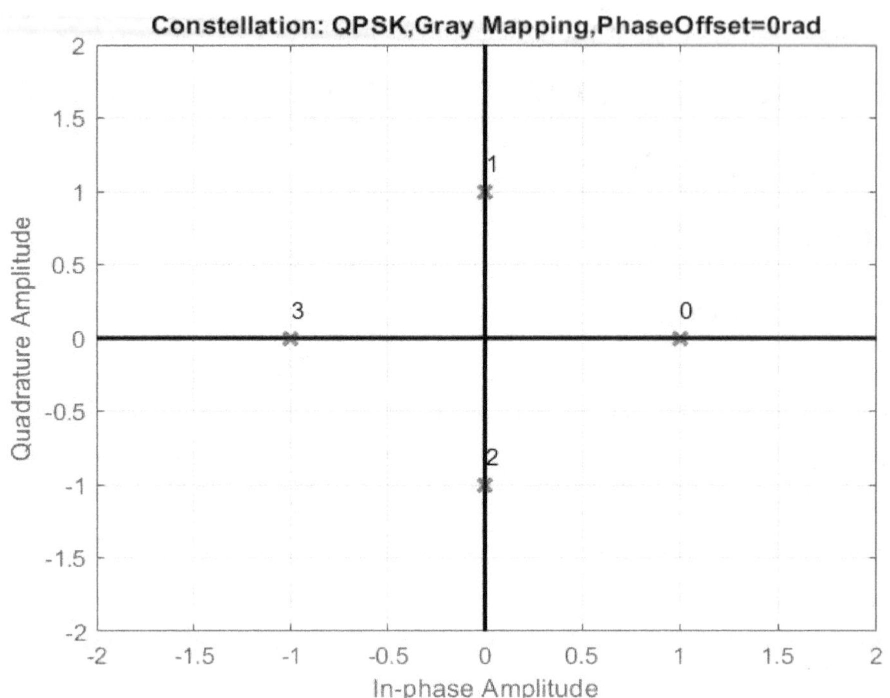

14.3 MATLAB CODE OF QUAFRATURE AMPLITUDE MODULATION TECHNIQUE WITH OUTPUT DIAGRAM:

Code a

```
M=256;
x=(0:M-1)';
y=qammod(x,M);
scatterplot(y)
```

Code b

```
M=16;
x=(0:M-1)';
y=qammod(x,M);
scatterplot(y)
```

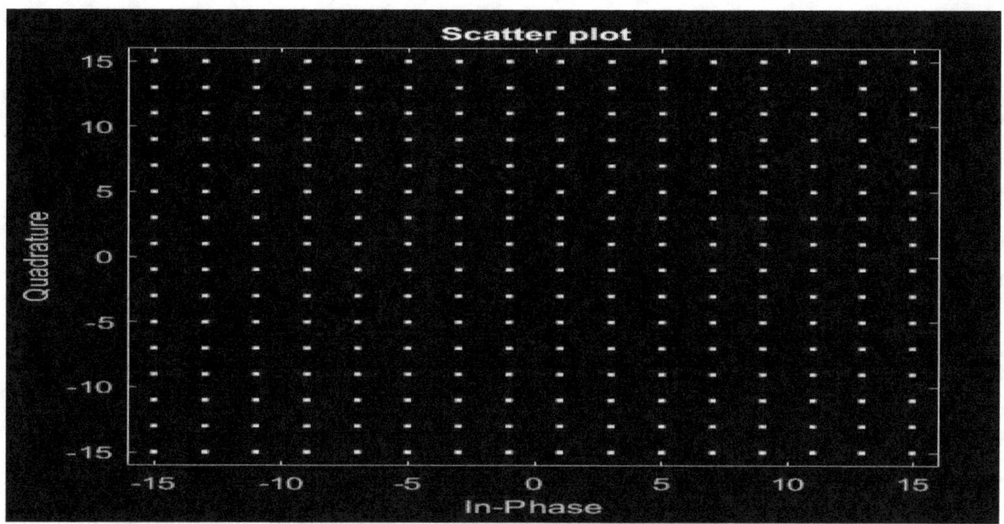

Scatter plot
Quadrature
In-Phase
15
10
5
0
-5
-10
-15
-15 -10 -5 0 5 10 15

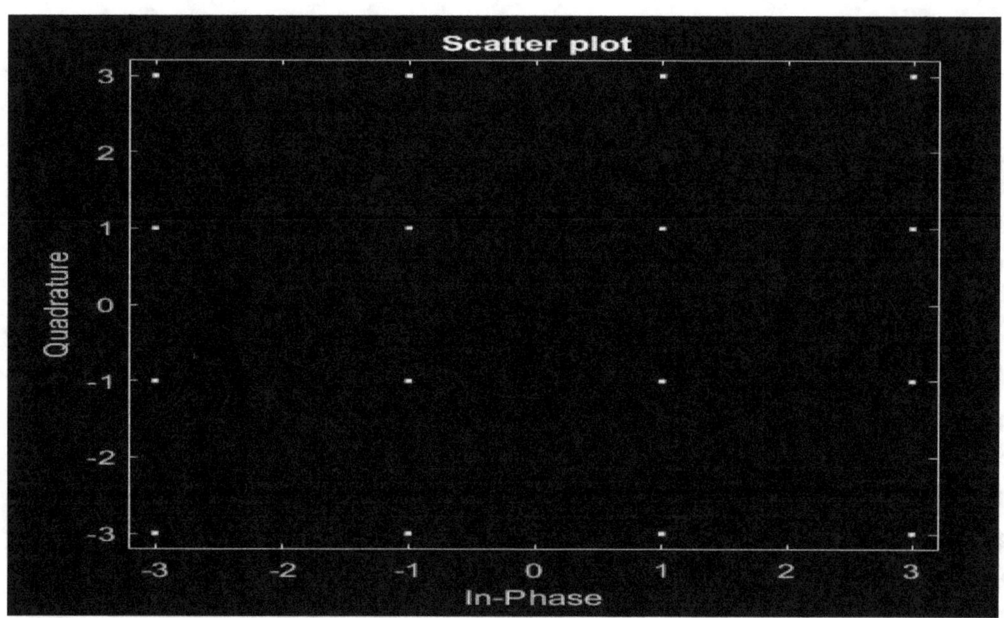

Scatter plot
Quadrature
In-Phase
3
2
1
0
-1
-2
-3
-3 -2 -1 0 1 2 3

CHAPTER-15

BASIC DISCUSSION OF INFORMATION THEORY

The amount of information received from an event is directly related to the uncertainly or inversely related to its probability of occurrence. So the information content of event is;

$I \sim \log(I/P)$ P=is the probability of occurrence

In general n equi-probable message are encoded by $\log_2(n)$ binary digits. The messages being equi-probable the probability (P) of any one message is $(1/n)$. Hence each message needs $\log_2(1/P)$ binary digits for encoding ;

Information content $I=K*\log_2(I/P)$

K=constant

$I=\log_2(I/P)$

15.1 INFORMATION SOURCES:

An information source is an object producing event, the outcome of which is selected at random according to some probability distribution. It is classified as memory less source. The former is one for which a current symbol depends on previous symbols-where the latter is one in which each symbol produced is independent of previous symbols.

15.2 Entropy:

The entropy (H) of s discrete random variable x is a measure of the amount of uncertainly associated with the value of x. The entropy is less when the uncertainly is more. It is expressed interms of average information per individual message.

The amount of information in message $m_1=I(m_1)=\log(1/P_1)$

Number of message $m_1=P_1*L$

Total information content in all m message=$P_1*L*\log(1/P_1)$

The amount of information in message $m_2=I(m_2)=\log(1/P_2)$

Total information content in all m_2 messages=$P_2*L*\log(1/P_2)$

Number of message $m_k=I(m_k)=\log(1/P_k)$

Total information in message in all $m_k=P_k*L*\log(I/P_k)$

Average information per message or Entropy(H) is;

$$H=I_{total}/L=P_1*\log(1/P_1)+P_2*\log(1/P_2)+P_3*\log(1/P_3)+\ldots\ldots\ldots+P_M*\log(1/P_M)$$

15.3 Rate of information:

If a message source generates messages at a rate of r messages per second, the rate of $_{infjormation}$ R is defined as the average number of bits of information per second.

Hence rate of information R is R=r*H bits/sec

15.4 Mutual of information:

Prior to the reception of a message in a real life communication system, the state of knowledge at the about a transmitted signal x_j is the probability that x_j would be selected for transmission;

$I(x_j : y_k)=-\log(P(x_j))=\log(P(x_j/y_k)/P(x_j))$

15.5 CHANNEL CAPACITY:

A suitable measure for transmission efficiency of information over a communication channel may be obtained by maximizing mutual information. Shanon has introduced channel capacity defined as the maximum of mutual information. It is the highest upper bound on the amount of information that can be readily transmitted over a communication channel

$$C=\max I(X;Y)$$

15.6 SHANON HEARTLEY LAW

The bandwidth and signal to noise ratio in communication is highlighted by shanon-heartly law. For an addition white Gaussian noise(AWGN) channel, the-channel output(Y) is given by the sum of the channel input (x) and the additive band-limited white Gaussian noise; the capacity C_s of such a channel is

$C_s=\max I(X;Y)=1/2*\log_2(1+S/N)$ bits/sample

Channel capacity C(b/s) of AWGN channel is $C=2*B*C_s=B*\log(1+S/N)$ **bps.**

15.7 LINE CODING

15.7.1 UNIPOLAR RZ AND NRZ:

If symbol '1' is transmitted then $x(t)=\{A; o<t<T_b/2 \| 0; T_b/2<t<T_b$

15.7.2 POLAR RZ AND NRZ:

If symbol '1' is transmitted then $x(t)=\{A/2 \; 0<=t<T_b/2\| 0 \; T_b/2<t<T_b$

If symbol '0' is transmitted then $x(t)=\{- A/2 \; 0<=t<T_b/2\| 0 \; T_b/2<t<T_b$

15.7.3 BIPOLAR NRZ:

In bipolar NRZ or alternate mark inversion (AMI) form, the successive '1''s are represented by pulses with alternative polarity and '0's are represented by no pulses.

15.7.4 SPLIT PHASE MANCHESTER:

If symbol '1' is transmitted then $x(t)= \{A/2 \; 0<=t<T_b/2\| 0 \; T_b/2<t<T_b$

If symbol '0' is transmitted then $x(t)= \{-A/2 \; 0<=t<T_b/2\| 0 \; T_b/2<t<T_b$

15.7.5 POLAR QUATERNAR NRZ:

MESSAGE COMBINATION	AMPLITUDE LEVEL
00	$-3A/2$
01	$-A/2$
01	$A/2$
11	$3A/2$

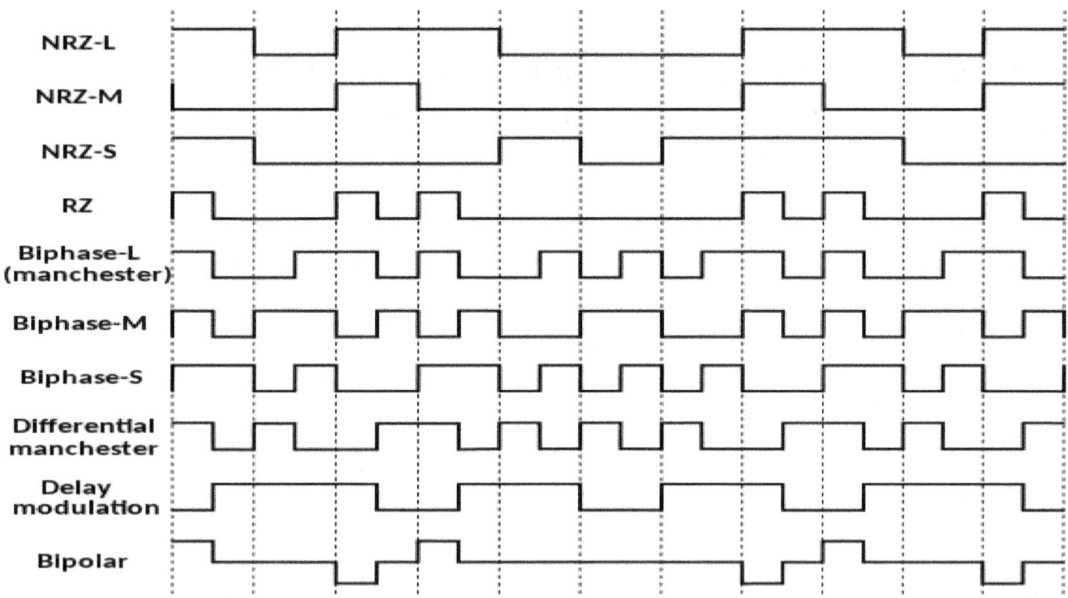

15.8 PARITY CHECK CODE:

The parity -check code is perhaps the simplest block code where the of check bits is 1, when in the check bit is such that the total number of 1's in the code word is even, it is called even parity check code and when the check bit is such that the total number of 1s is odd in the code word.

Message	Code for even parity	check bit bit	code for odd parity	check bit
001011	001011	1	001011	0
100010	100010	0	100010	1

15.9 CYCLIC CODE:

A subclass of linear block code facilating the design of higher order correcting codes is the cyclic code. Here encoding and syndrome calculator is the cyclic code. Here encoding and syndrome calculations are easily implemented using simple shift registers.

a. All burst error of length (n-k) or less.
b. All fractions of burst error of length equal (n-k+1) the fraction being $1-2^{(n-k+1)}$.
c. A fraction of burst error, of length greater than (n-k+1) ; the fraction being $1- 2^{-(n-k-1)}$

d. **All combination of d_{min} -1 or less errors.**

e. **All burst error pattern with odd number of errors; g(x) for the code having even number of non-zero coefficients.**

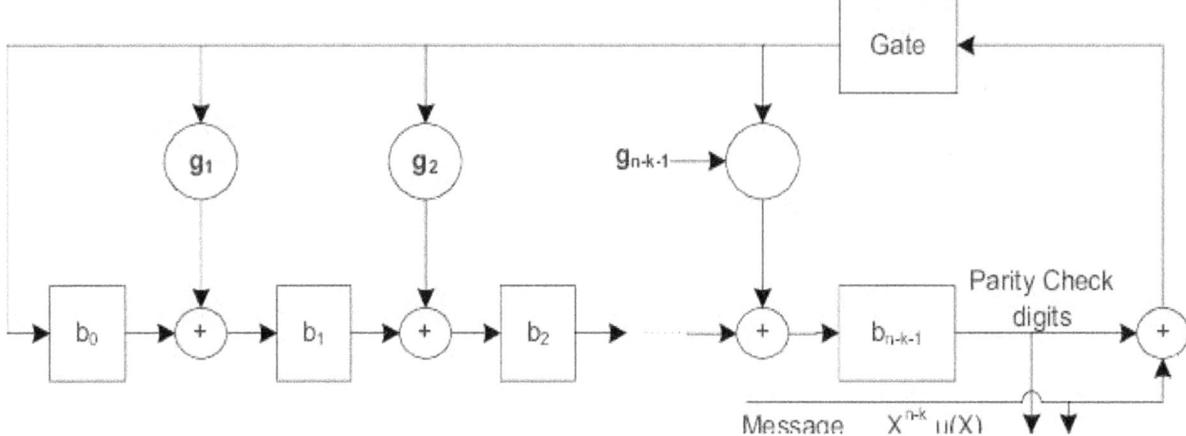

15.10 INTER SYMBOL INTERFERENCE:

The dispersive nature of the communication channel or the imperfections in the overall frequency response of the system gives rise to a phenomenon called inter-symbol interference in digital baseband transmission. In practice, the frequency components present in a short pulse (duration T_b) to be transmitted through a band-limited system are differentially attenuated and delayed which causes pulse dispersion at the output over an interval larger than T_b seconds.

Effect of ISI:

> **a. Decode operation at the receiver for the transmitted bit is made absence of ISI and noise.**

> **b. Errors in decision are introduced at the receiver output to presence to presence of ISI. Thus reception of logic 1 or 0 may not be correctly made at the receiver.**

Remedy to reduce ISI

> **a. Use of sync pulse instead of rectangular pulse preferred to reduce ISI.**
> **b. The frequency response of the filter can be modified with different roll of factors.**

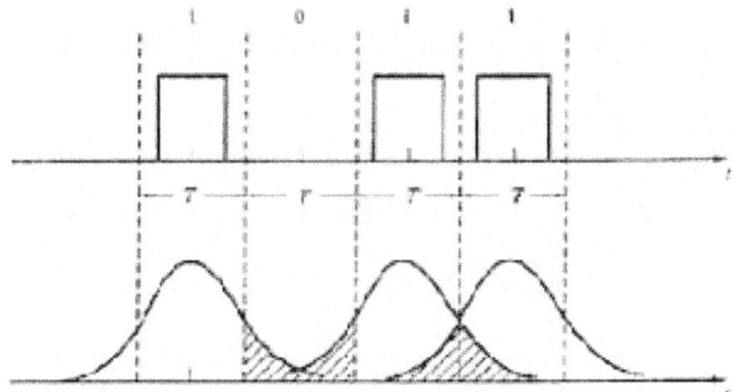

<u>Inter symbolic interference pattern</u>

15.11 EYE PATTERN:

Eye pattern in basically a pattern displayed on the CRO screen with shape resembling that of a human eye. It represents a pictorial study of ISI and its effects on PCM or data communication system. The received signal is applied to vertical deflecting plates while a saw-tooth wave at the transmission symbol rate to the horizontal deflection plates. The interior part of the eye opening. It provides lot of information about system performance. The reduction in the eye opening indication more ISI and vice versa while complete eye closure.

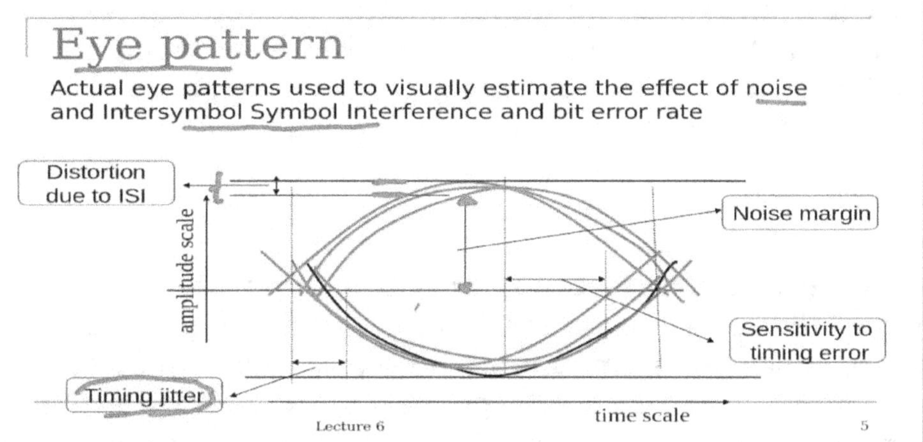

15.12 REGENERATIVE REPEATER:

A regenerative repeater is an amplifier that boosts the signal strength along with the transmission media. Regenerative repeater detects and regenerates an original strength signal which is free from noise in digital communication, A regenerative repeater amplifies and reconstructs such a badly distorted digital signal and develops a nearly perfect replica of the original at its output. Regenerative repeaters are an essential key to digital

transmission in that we could say that the "noise stops at the repeater.

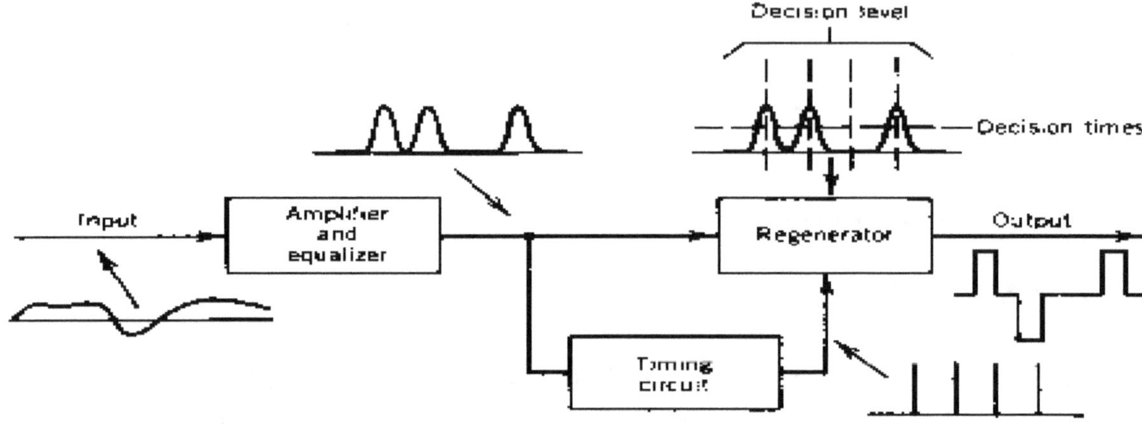

CHAPTER-16

QANTISATION THEORY AND DELTA MODULATION TECHNIQUE

The digitization of analog signals involves the rounding off of the values which are approximately equal to the analog values. The method of sampling chooses a few points on the analog signal and then these points are joined to round off the value to a near stabilized value. Such a process is called as Quantization.

16.1 Quantizing an Analog Signal

The analog-to-digital converters perform this type of function to create a series of digital values out of the given analog signal. The following figure represents an analog signal. This signal to get converted into digital, has to undergo sampling and quantizing. Both sampling and quantization result in the loss of information. The quality of a Quantizer output depends upon the number of quantization levels used. The discrete amplitudes of the quantized output are called as representation levels or reconstruction levels. The spacing between the two adjacent representation levels is called a quantum or step-size.

The following figure shows the resultant quantized signal which is the digital form for the given analog signal.

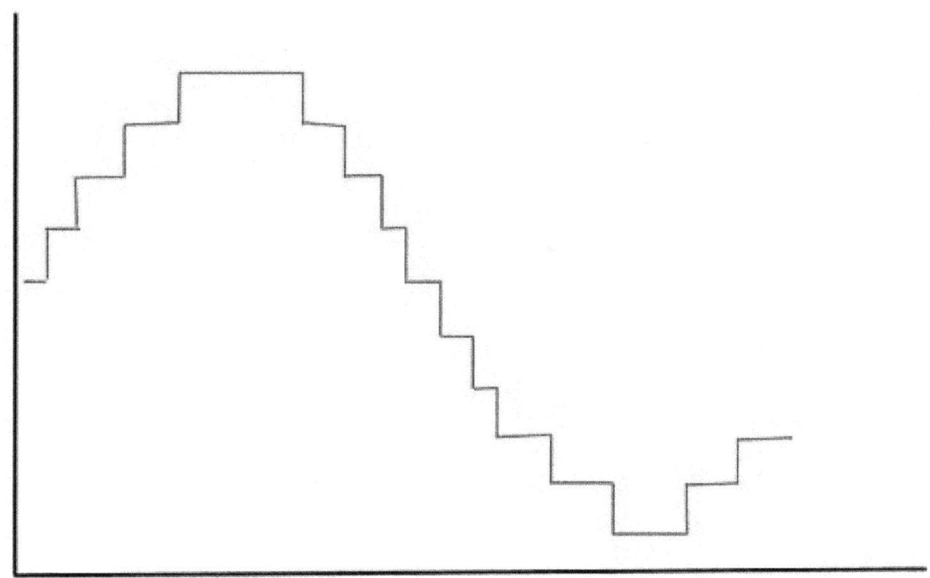

This is also called as **Stair-case** waveform, in accordance with its shape.

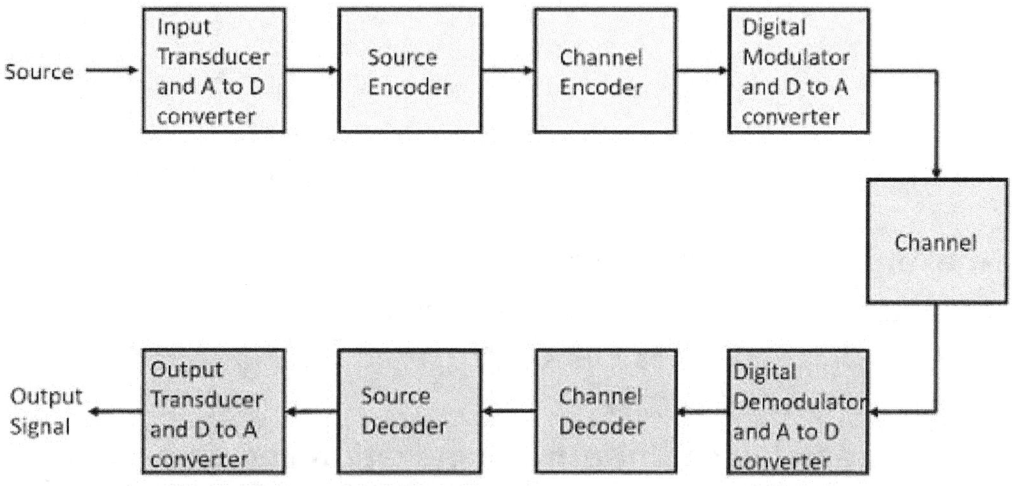

16.2 Uniform Quantization

The quantization levels or the differences between each discrete value is uniform. The relation between such quantum levels is mostly arithmetic. There are two types of uniform quantization which are known as mid-rise and mid-tread types. The difference between them is that the mid-rise type has its origin in the middle of a staircase-like graph, whereas the mid-tread type has its origin in the middle of a tread of a staircase-like graph.

Types of Uniform Quantization

- Mid-rise type Uniform Quantization: The discrete quantized signal originates from the midpoint of the ascending portion of the stair-like graph, often referred to as the "rise."
- Mid-tread type Uniform Quantization: The discrete quantized signal has its starting point positioned at the center of the flat portion, known as the "tread," within the stair-like graph.

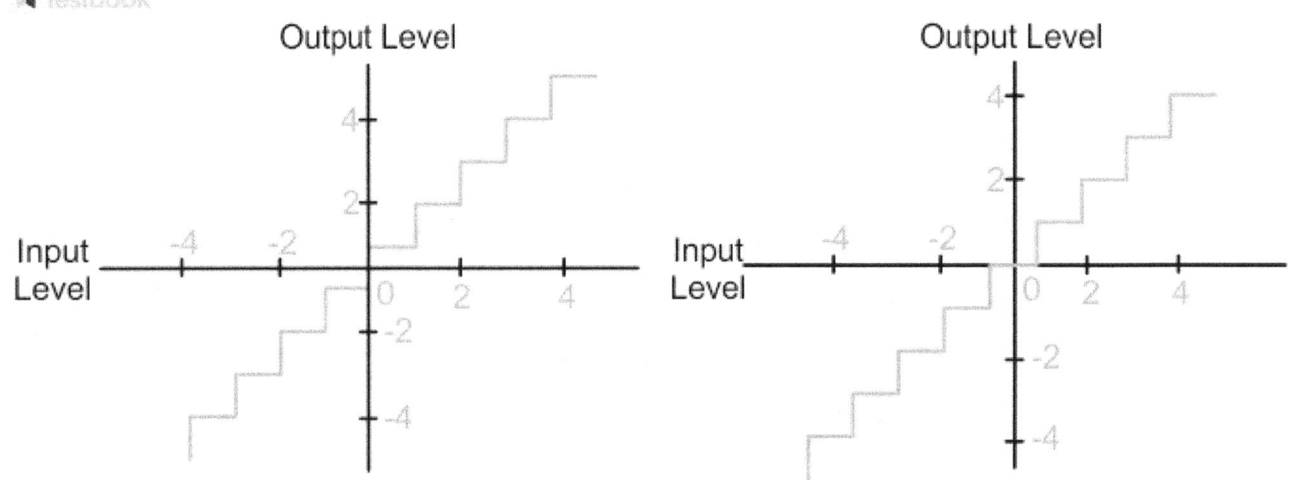

Mid-Rise type Uniform Quantization   Mid-Tread type Uniform Quantization

16.3 Non-Uniform Quantization

The quantization levels or the differences between each discrete value are not uniform. These levels are unequal and mostly are related to a logarithmic curve.

16.4 Difference between Uniform Quantization and Non-uniform Quantization

The following table discusses the difference between uniform and non-uniform quantization.

Parameter	Uniform Quantization	Non-uniform Quantization
Quantization levels	Equally spaced quantization levels	Unequally spaced quantization levels
Step size	Same step size between all quantization levels	Variable step sizes between quantization levels

Distribution of input data	Not accounted for input data distribution	Accounts for input data distribution
Quantization error	Quantization error is uniform across all inputs	Lower quantization error for frequently occurring inputs
Complexity	Simple to implement	More complex to implement
Applications	Used when input distribution is uniform	Used when input distribution is non-uniform, like image/audio signals

16.4 Companding

Companding is a type of non-uniform quantization and is used to increase the strength of the weak signals. It reduces the data rate of the input signal by varying the gap between the two adjacent quantization levels. The unequal quantization level makes it similar to the non-uniform quantization process.

Companding is created from the combination of two words, compression and expanding. The signal is passed through the compressor at the transmitting end while it is passed through the expander at the receiving end. The compressor compresses the signal and improves the quality of transmission. But, it introduces distortion in the signal. The expander is used at the receiving end to undo the distortion introduced by the compressor. The inverse distortions of the two processes (compression and expanding) help in generating the output signal without distortion.

The input-output characteristics of the expander are the reverse as compared to the compressor, as shown below:

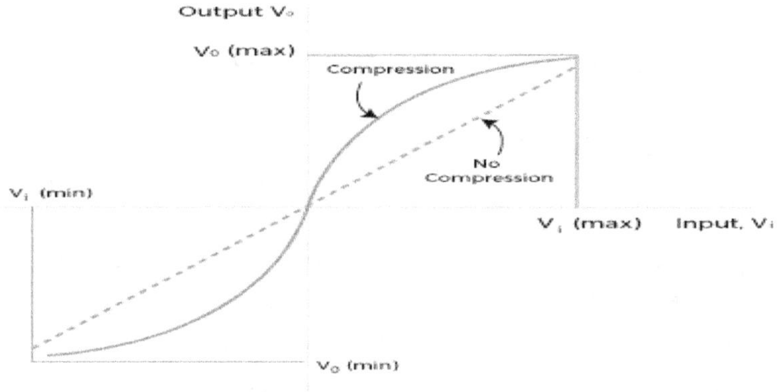

16.5 DELTA MODULATION

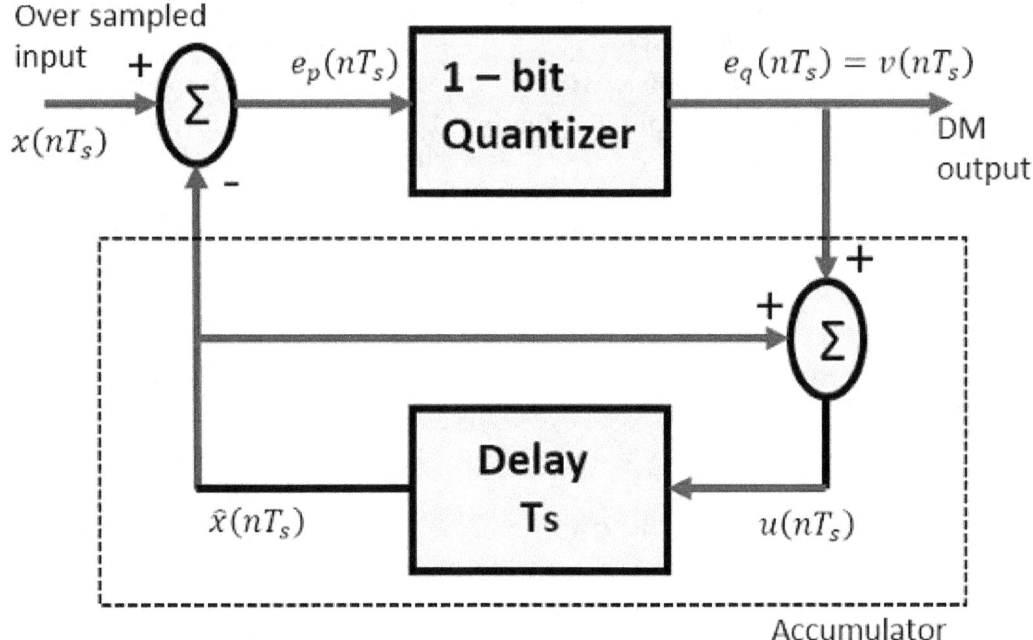

The type of modulation, where the sampling rate is much higher and in which the stepsize after quantization is of a smaller value Δ, such a modulation is termed as delta modulation.

Features of Delta Modulation

Following are some of the features of delta modulation.

- An over-sampled input is taken to make full use of the signal correlation.
- The quantization design is simple.
- The input sequence is much higher than the Nyquist rate.
- The quality is moderate.
- The design of the modulator and the demodulator is simple.
- The stair-case approximation of output waveform.
- The step-size is very small, i.e., Δ deltadelta.
- The bit rate can be decided by the user.
- This involves simpler implementation.

Delta Modulation is a simplified fThe predictor circuit in DPCM is replaced by a simple delay circuit in DM.

From the above diagram, we have the notations as −

- $x(nT_s)$ = over sampled input
- $e_p(nT_s)$ = summer output and quantizer input
- $e_q(nT_s)$ = quantizer output = $v(nT_s)$
- $x^{\wedge}(nT_s)$ = output of delay circuit
- $u(nT_s)$ = input of delay circuit

orm of DPCM technique, also viewed as 1-bit DPCM scheme. **As the sampling interval is reduced, the signal correlation will be higher.**

The Delta Modulator comprises of a 1-bit quantizer and a delay circuit along with two summer circuits. Following is the block diagram of a delta modulator.

The delta modulation has two major drawbacks as under :
1. Slope overload distortion
2. Granular or idle noise

Now, we will discuss these two drawbacks in detail.

a. Slope Overload Distortion

This distortion arises because of large dynamic range of the input signal.

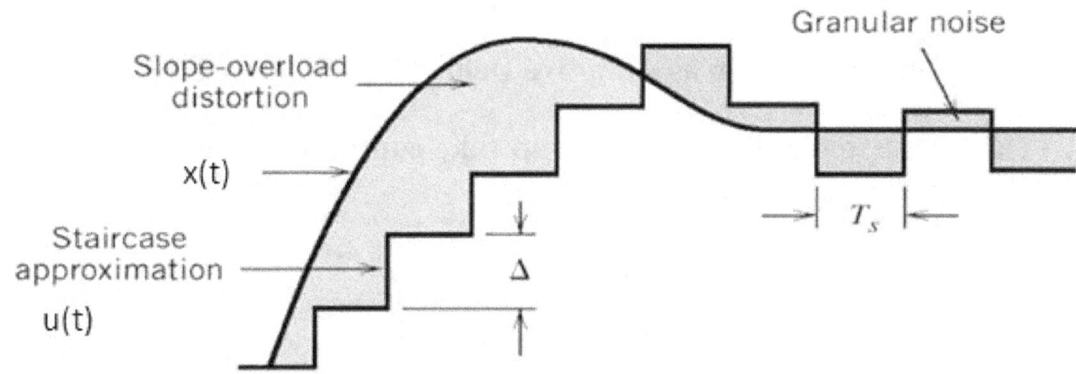

Fig.1: Quantization Errors in Delta Modulation

We can observe from fig.1 , the rate of rise of input signal x(t) is so high that the staircase signal can not approximate it, the step size 'Δ' becomes too small for staircase signal u(t) to follow the step segment of x(t).

Hence, there is a large error between the staircase approximated signal and the original input signal x(t).

This error or noise is known as slope overload distortion .
To reduce this error, the step size must be increased when slope of signal x(t) is high.

b.Granular or Idle Noise

Granular or Idle noise occurs when the step size is too large compared to small variation in the input signal.

This means that for very small variations in the input signal, the staircase signal is changed by large amount (Δ) because of large step size.

Fig.1 shows that when the input signal is almost flat , the staircase signal u(t) keeps on oscillating by $\pm\Delta$ around the signal.

The error between the input and approximated signal is called granular noise. The solution to this problem is to make the step size small .

16.6 Solution

In order to overcome the quantization errors due to slope overload and granular noise, the step size (Δ) is made adaptive to variations in the input signal x(t).
Particularly in the steep segment of the signal x(t), the step size is increased. And the step is decreased when the input is varying slowly.

This method is known as Adaptive Delta Modulation (ADM).

The adaptive delta modulators can take continuous changes in step size or discrete changes in step size.

CHAPTER-17

CONCLUSION

Here author has displayed only 4 different types of mat-lab codes of mat-lab related programming technology for theoretical understanding purpose of academic students for semesters. Now several more theoretical concepts are there related to digital communication subjects; students may understand those subjects from other books the same author of analog and advanced communication where propagation of wave theory has been described with examples. If any further extension is required then you may consult some advanced books related digital communication theory related to several more chapters because here in this book author has described some commonly analysable chapters for the students in terms of semesters.

[ANNEXTURE BOOK-3]

LABORATORY HANDBOOK OF C PROGRAMMING LANGUAGE FOR PRACTICE PURPOSE

ABSTRACT

This handbook is dedicated for laboratory for purpose only; graduate engineering students learn C or C++ programming in their first year of engineering study; for theatrical purpose author has explained some very important chapters which are very much related to understand C programming concept. In this handbook author has displayed many simple but logical programming of C or C++ with corresponding output for the laboratory purpose of all branches of engineering students. Students can use all the codes in many other C programming also.

BASIC THEORICAL DISCUSSION

SL NO	CHAPTERS	PAGE NO
1	INTRODUCTION	106
2	WHAT IS C PROGRAMMING	106-107
3	SYNTAX USED IN C PROGRAMMING	107-108
4	DEFINITION VARIABLE IN C PROGRAMMING	108-109
5	WHAT IS STRING AND POINTER	109-110
6	DEFINITION OF FOR LOOP	110
7	DEFINITION OF IF-ELSE CONDITION	111
8	DEFINITION OF WHILE LOOP	111
9	DEFINITION OF SWITCH CASE	111

C PROGRAMMING FOR LABORATORY PRACTICE

SL NO	NAME OF PROGRAMMING	PAGE NO
1	ARITHMATICAL ADDITION,SUBSTRACTION, MULTIPLICATION, DIVISION [DECIMAL, WHOLE DIGIT]	112-113
2	CHECK LEAP YEAR OR NOT	113
3	CHECK PRIME NUMBER OR NOT	114
4	CHECK POSITIVE OR NEGETIVE NUMBER	114
5	CHECK ODD OR EVEN NUMBER	115
6	GREATER BETWEEN TWO DIFFERENT NUMBERS	115-116
7	COMPLEMENT OF ANY NUMBER	116
8	CALCULATION OF GROSS SALARY OF AN EMPLOYEE	116-117
9	ENTER 5 MARKS CALCULATE TOTAL AND AVARAGE	117-118
10	WHILE LOOP PROGRAMMING EXAMPLES	119-120
11	IF ELSE LOOP PROGRAMMING EXAMPLES	120-123
12	EXAMPLE OF SWITCH CASE	123-128
13	FORMATION OF PYRAMID TRIANGLE	128-129

BASIC THEORICAL DISCUSSION

CHAPTER-1

INTRODUCTION

In engineering subjects graduate and diploma engineering students need to learn very common subjects in their 1ˢᵗ year as basic subjects; among them C programming is a very common subject that students need to learn in engineering; till now author has used mat-lab code as a common engineering tool for engineering purpose now author has decided to show the students how to learn C programming for laboratory practice purpose; here author has Dev-C++ software for programming purpose. So many programming's are available but for the time being author has displayed very important programming for practice in laboratory of C programming technology.

CHAPTER-2

WHAT IS C PROGRAMMING

The C programming language is a general-purpose, operating system-agnostic, and procedural language that supports structured programming and provides low-level access to the system memory. Dennis Ritchie invented C language in 1972 at AT&T (then called Bell Laboratory), where it was implemented in the UNIX system on DEC PDP II. It was also the successor of the B programming language invented by Ken Thompson. C was designed to overcome the problems encountered by BASIC, B, and BPCL programming languages. By 1980, C became the most popular language for mainframes, microcomputers, and minicomputers

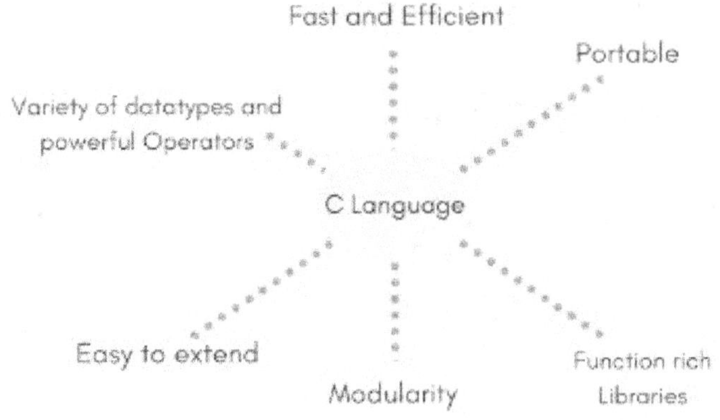

2.1 Features of C Programming

Loved by programmers for doing low-level coding and embedded programming, C has found its way gradually into the semiconductor, hardware, and storage industries. The most important features provided by the C programming languages include:

- It has inbuilt functions and operators that can solve virtually any complex problem

- C is the combination of both low level (assembly) and high-level programming languages; also, it can be used to write an application and interact with low-level system memory and hardware

- It can be written on practically any operating system and even works in most handheld devices

- Programs written in C are speedy due to the support provided by its datatypes and operators

- It is easily extendable, as C++ was derived from C with additions like OOPS and other features

- The functions and operators are supported by the libraries provided by the programming language itself.

CHAPTER-3

COMMON SYNTAX USED IN C PROGRAMMING

```c
#include <stdio.h>
int main()
int var; [integer variable]
char a;  [character variable]
float a; [float variable]
printf("Name: ");
scanf("Name: ");
```

```
    return 0;
    for(int=0;i<5;i++)
```

CHAPTER-4

DEFINITION VARIABLE IN C PROGRAMMING

There are 3 aspects of defining a variable:

1. **Variable Declaration**
2. **Variable Definition**
3. **Variable Initializatio**
   a. Variable Declaration

Variable declaration in C tells the compiler about the existence of the variable with the given name and data type.When the variable is declared, an entry in symbol table is created and memory will be allocated at the time of initialization of the variable.

   b. Variable Definition

In the definition of a C variable, the compiler allocates some memory and some value to it. A defined variable will contain some random garbage value till it is not initialized.

Example

```
int var;

char var2;
```

Note: Most of the modern C compilers declare and define the variable in single step. Although we can declare a variable in C by using extern keyword, it is not required in most of the cases. To know more about variable declaration and definition, click here.

   c.Variable Initialization

Initialization of a variable is the process where the user assigns some meaningful value to the variable when creating the variable.

Example

```
int var = 10;   // variable declaration and definition (i.e. Vairable Initialization)
```

Difference between Variable Initialization and Assignment

Initialization occurs when a variable is first declared and assigned an initial value. This usually happens during the declaration of the variable. On the other hand, assignment involves setting or updating the value of an already declared variable, and this can happen multiple times after the initial initialization.

Example

```
int a=10;      //Variable initialization

a=10;          //assignment
```

CHAPTER-5
WHAT IS STRING AND POINTER

String is a data type that stores the sequence of characters in an array. Every string terminates with a null character (\0), indicating its termination. A pointer to a string in C can be used to point to the base address of the string array, and its value can be dereferenced to get the value of the string, Pointers, serving as variables that store memory addresses, are instrumental in manipulating memory efficiently. Strings, on the other hand, are arrays of characters terminated by a null character (\0), used extensively for handling text. Strings are used for storing text/characters. For example, "Hello World" is a string of characters. Unlike many other programming languages, C does not have a String type to easily create string variables.

```c
#include <stdio.h>
int main()
{
    char name[30];
    printf("Enter name: ");
    fgets(name, sizeof(name), stdin);  // read string
    printf("Name: ");
    puts(name);      // display string
```

```
    return 0;
}
```

CHAPTER-6
DEFINITION OF FOR LOOP

1. i is initialized to 1.
2. The test expression i < 11 is evaluated. Since 1 less than 11 is true, the body of for loop is executed. This will print the 1 (value of i) on the screen.
3. The update statement ++i is executed. Now, the value of i will be 2. Again, the test expression is evaluated to true, and the body of for loop is executed. This will print 2 (value of i) on the screen.
4. Again, the update statement ++i is executed and the test expression i < 11 is evaluated. This process goes on until i becomes 11.

When i becomes 11, i < 11 will be false, and the for loop terminates. Here is one example of for loop;

```c
// Print numbers from 1 to 10

#include <stdio.h>

int main() {

  int i;

  for (i = 1; i < 11; ++i)

  {

    printf("%d ", i);

  }

  return 0;

}

[ 1 2 3 4 5 6 7 8 9 10]
```

CHAPTER-7
DEFINITION OF IF-ELSE CONDITION

In C programming, the if-else statement is called a conditional statement. They are used in the decision-making process. When there are multiple conditions, programmers can use these statements to drive the output.

If-else is often used in pairs where the if statement lies above the else statement. The compiler will first check the "if " statement, and go to the else part only when the "if" condition fails.

If the "if" condition satisfies, the "if " statement will execute. When "if " returns False, the else statement body will execute.

CHAPTER-8
DEFINITION OF WHILE LOOP

A while loop is a control flow statement that allows code to be executed repeatedly based on a given Boolean condition. The while loop can be thought of as a repeating if statement.

CHAPTER-9
DEFINITION OF SWITCH CASE

Switch case statement evaluates a given expression and based on the evaluated value(matching a certain condition), it executes the statements associated with it. Basically, it is used to perform different actions based on different conditions(cases).

- Switch case statements follow a selection-control mechanism and allow a value to change control of execution.
- They are a substitute for long _if statements_ that compare a variable to several integral values.
- The switch statement is a multiway branch statement. It provides an easy way to dispatch execution to different parts of code based on the value of the expression.

In C, the switch case statement is used for executing one condition from multiple conditions. It is similar to an if-else-if ladder.

C PROGRAMMING FOR LABORATORY PRACTICE

CHAPTER-1

ARITHMATICAL-ADDITION,SUBSTRACTION,MULTIPLICATION,
DIVISION [DECIMAL, WHOLE DIGIT]

1.1 PROGRAMMING CODE OF WHOLE DIGIT:

```c
#include<stdio.h>
int main()
{
    int a, b, c1,c2,c3,c4,c5;
    printf("enter the first number",a);
    scanf("%d",&a);
    printf("enter the second number",b);
    scanf("%d",&b);
    c1=a+b;
    printf("the sum is%d\n",c1);
    c2=a-b;
    printf("the difference is%d\n",c2);
    c3=a*b;
    printf("the mutiplicstion is%d\n",c3);
    c4=a/b;
    printf("the division is%d\n",c4);
    c5=a%b;
    printf("the reminder is%d\n",c5);
    return 0;
}
```

OUTPUT

```
enter the first number17
enter the second number6
the sum is23
the difference is11
the mutiplicstion is102
the division is2
the reminder is5
```

1.2 PROGRAMMING CODE OF DECIMAL DIGIT:

```c
#include<stdio.h>
int main()
{
```

```c
    float a, b, c1,c2,c3,c4,c5;
    printf("enter the first number",a);
    scanf("%f",&a);
    printf("enter the second number",b);
    scanf("%f",&b);
    c1=a+b;
    printf("the sum is%f\n",c1);
    c2=a-b;
    printf("the difference is%f\n",c2);
    c3=a*b;
    printf("the mutiplicstion is%f\n",c3);
    c4=a/b;
    printf("the division is%f\n",c4);
    return 0;
}
```

OUTPUT

```
enter the first number15.6
enter the second number5.2
the sum is20.799999
the difference is10.400001
the mutiplicstion is81.120003
the division is3.000000
```

CHAPTER-2
CHECK LEAP YEAR OR NOT

9.1 PROGRAMMING CODE:

```c
#include<stdio.h>
int main()
{
    int a;
    printf("enter the year",a)
    scanf("%d",&a);
    ((a%400==0)&&(a%400==0||a%100==0))?printf("it   is   a
leap year"):printf("it is not a leap year");
    return 0;
}
```

9.2 OUTPUT:

```
enter the year2000
it is a leap year
```

CHAPTER-3
CHECK PRIME NUMBER OR NOT

10.1 PROGRAMMING CODE:

```c
#include<stdio.h>
int main()
{
    int a;
    printf("enter the digit:",a);
    scanf("%d",&a);
    if(a%2==0)
    printf("the number is prime number");
    else
    printf("the number is not prime number");
    return 0;
}
```

10.2 OUTPUT:

```
enter the digit:12
the number is prime number
```

CHAPTER-4
CHECK POSITIVE OR NEGETIVE NUMBER

4.1 PROGRAMMING CODE:

```c
#include<stdio.h>
int main()
{
    int a;
    printf("enter any number:",a);
    scanf("%d",&a);
    (a>0)?printf("positive"):printf("negetive");
    return 0;
}
```

4.2 OUTPUT:

```
enter any number:12
positive
enter any number:-57
negetive
```

CHAPTER-5
CHECK ODD OR EVEN NUMBER

5.1 PROGRAMMING CODE:

```c
#include<stdio.h>
int main()
{
    int a;
    printf("enter any number:",a);
    scanf("%d",&a);
    (a%2==0)?printf("even"):printf("odd");
    return 0;
}
```

5.2 OUTPUT:

```
enter any number:12
even
enter any number:27
odd
```

CHAPTER-6
GREATER BETWEEN TWO DIFFERENT NUMBERS

6.1 PROGRAMMING CODE:

```c
#include<stdio.h>
int main()
{
    int a,b;
    printf("enter any number:",a);
    scanf("%d",&a);
    printf("enter any number:",b);
    scanf("%d",&b);
    if(a>b)
    {
    printf("first number is greater");
    }
    else
    {
    printf("second number is greater");
    }
    return 0;
```

```
}
```

    6.2 OUTPUT:
    enter any number:12
    enter any number:16
    second number is greater
    enter any number:67
    enter any number:58
    first number is greater

CHAPTER-7

COMPLEMENT OF ANY NUMBER

7.1 PROGRAMMING CODE:

```c
#include<stdio.h>
int main()
{
    int a,b;
    printf("enter any number:",a);
    scanf("%d",&a);
    b=~a;
    printf("the complement of the number%d\n",b);
    return 0;
}
```

7.2 OUTPUT:
enter any number:23
the complement of the number-24

CHAPTER-8

CALCULATION OF GROSS SALARY OF AN EMPLOYEE

8.1 PROGRAMMING CODE:

```c
#include<stdio.h>
int main()
{
    int x,TA,DA,HRA,MEDICAL, TOTAL;
    printf("enter the salary:",x);
    scanf("%d",&x);
    TA=.2*x;
    DA=.15*x;
    HRA=.1*x;
```

```c
    MEDICAL=.08*x;
    TOTAL=TA+DA+HRA+MEDICAL+x;
    printf("the total amount of the salary is%d\n",TOTAL);
    printf("the total DA of the salary is%d\n",DA);
    printf("the total HRA of the salary is%d\n",HRA);
    printf("the total TA of the salary is%d\n",TA);
    printf("the      total      MEDICAL      of      the      salary
is%d\n",MEDICAL);
    return 0;
}
```

8.2 OUTPUT:

```
enter the salary:18000
the total amount of the salary is27540
the total DA of the salary is2700
the total HRA of the salary is1800
the total TA of the salary is3600
the total MEDICAL of the salary is1440
```

CHAPTER-9

ENTER 5 MARKS CALCULATE TOTAL AND AVARAGE

9.1 PROGRAMMING CODE:

```c
#include<stdio.h>
int main()
{
    int a,b,c,d,e,avg,t;
    printf("enter the first marks:",a);
    scanf("%d",&a);
    printf("enter the second marks:",b);
    scanf("%d",&b);
    printf("enter the third marks:",c);
    scanf("%d",&c);
    printf("enter the fourth marks:",d);
    scanf("%d",&d);
    printf("enter the fifth marks:",e);
    scanf("%d",&e);
    t=a+b+c+d+e;
```

```c
    printf("the total marks is%d\n",t);
    avg=(a+b+c+d+e)/5;
    printf("the average marks is%d\n",avg);
    if(avg>=90)
    {
        printf("the grade is AA");
    }
    else if(avg>=80)
    {
        printf("the grade is A+");
    }
    else if(avg>=70)
    {
        printf("the grade is A");
    }
    else if(avg>=50)
    {
        printf("the grade is B");
    }
    else if(avg>=40)
    {
        printf("the grade is C");
    }
    else
    {
        printf("the grade is D");
    }

}
9.2 output:
enter the first marks:56
enter the second marks:67
enter the third marks:78
enter the fourth marks:93
enter the fifth marks:64
the total marks is358
the average marks is71
the grade is A
```

CHAPTER-10

WHILE LOOP PROGRAMMING EXAMPLES

10.1 PROGRAMMING CODE 1:

```c
#include<stdio.h>
int main()
{
   int a=1,n;
   printf("enter any number");
   scanf("%d",&n);
   while(a<=n)
   {
       if(a%2==0)
       {
            printf("%d\n",a);
       }
       a++;
   }
   return 0;
}
```

10.2 OUTPUT:

```
enter any number9
2
4
6
8
```

10.3 PROGRAMMING CODE 2:

```c
#include<stdio.h>
int main()
{
   int a=1,n;
   printf("enter any number");
   scanf("%d",&n);
   while(a<=n)
```

```c
    {
        if(a%2!=0)
        {
            printf("%d\n",a);
        }
        a++;
    }
    return 0;
}
```

10.4 OUTPUT:

```
enter any number7
1
3
5
7
```

CHAPTER-11

IF ELSE LOOP PROGRAMMING EXAMPLES

11.1 PROGRAMMING CODE 1:

```c
#include<stdio.h>

int main()

{

    int a,b,c;

    printf("enter the first side:",a);

    scanf("%d",&a);

    printf("enter the second side:",b);

    scanf("%d",&b);

    printf("enter the third side:",c);

    scanf("%d",&c);

    if(a==b&&b==c&&c==a)
```

```c
        {
                printf("equilatral triangle");
        }
        else if(a==b||b==c||c==a)
        {
                printf("isoscales triangle");
        }
        else
        {
                printf("scalene triangle");
        }
}
```

11.2 OUTPUT :

enter the first side:7

enter the second side:7

enter the third side:7

equilatral triangle

enter the first side:7

enter the second side:8

enter the third side:8

isoscales triangle

11.3 PROGRAMMING CODE 2:

```c
#include<stdio.h>
```

```c
int main()
{
        int a,b,c;

        printf("enter the first angle:",a);

        scanf("%d",&a);

        printf("enter the second angle:",b);

        scanf("%d",&b);

        printf("enter the third angle:",c);

        scanf("%d",&c);

        if(a+b+c==180)

        {
                printf("valid triangle");
        }
        else if(a<90&&b<90&&c<90)

        {
                printf("acute triangle");
        }
        else if (a==90||b==90||c==90)

        {
                printf("right angled triangle");
        }
        else

        {
                printf("obtuse triangle");
```

}

}

11.4 OUTPUT:

enter the first angle:78

enter the second angle:42

enter the third angle:60

valid triangle

CHAPTER-12

EXAMPLE OF SWITCH CASE

12.1 PROGRAMMING CODE 1:

```c
#include<stdio.h>
int main()
{
    int a,b,c,n;
    printf("enter your choice");
    scanf("%d",&n);
    if(n==1)
    {
        printf("enter the first number:",a);
        scanf("%d",&a);
        printf("enter the second number:",b);
        scanf("%d",&b);
```

```c
        c=a+b;

        printf("the result of addition is%d\n",c);

}

else if(n==2)

{

        printf("enter the first number:",a);

        scanf("%d",&a);

        printf("enter the second number:",b);

        scanf("%d",&b);

        c=a-b;

        printf("the result of substraction is%d\n",c);

}

else if(n==3)

{

printf("enter the first number:",a);

        scanf("%d",&a);

        printf("enter the second number:",b);

        scanf("%d",&b);

        c=a*b;

        printf("the result of multiplication is%d\n",c);

}

else if(n==4)
```

```c
{
        printf("enter the first number:",a);

            scanf("%d",&a);

            printf("enter the second number:",b);

            scanf("%d",&b);

            c=a/b;

            printf("the result of division is%d\n",c);

    }

    else

    {

            printf("wrong choice");

    }

}
```

12.2 OUTPUT

enter your choice2

enter the first number:24

enter the second number:78

the result of substraction is-54

12.3 PROGRAMMING CODE 2:

```c
#include<stdio.h>
```

```c
int main()
{
    char a,n;
    printf("enter the character:");
    scanf("%c",&n);
    if((n>='a'&&n<='z')||(n>='A'&& n<='Z'))
    switch(n)
    {
        case 'a':
                printf("character is vowel");
                break;
        case 'e':
                printf("character is vowel");
                break;

        case 'i':
                printf("character is vowel");
                break;
        case 'o':
                printf("character is vowel");
                break;
        case 'u':
                printf("character is vowel");
```

```c
            break;
        case 'A':
            printf("character is vowel");
            break;
        case 'E':
            printf("character is vowel");
            break;
        case 'I':
            printf("character is vowel");
            break;
        case 'O':
            printf("character is vowel");
            break;
        case 'U':
            printf("character is vowel");
            break;
            return 0;
    }
}
```

12.4. OUTPUT:

enter the character:A

character is vowel

enter the character:a

character is vowel

CHAPTER-13

FORMATION OF PYRAMID TRIANGLE

13.1 PROGRAMMING CODE:

```c
#include<stdio.h>
int main()
{
      int i,space,rows,k=0;
      printf("enter the number of rows:");
      scanf("%d",&rows);
      for(i= 1;i<= rows; ++i,k= 0)
      {
      for(space=1;space<=rows-i;++space)
      {
      printf(" ");
}
while(k!=2*i-1)
{
      printf("*");
      ++k;
}
printf("\n");
      }
      return 0;
```

}

12.2 OUTPUT

enter the number of rows:9

```
        *
       ***
      *****
     *******
    *********
   ***********
  *************
 ***************
*****************
```

CONCLUSION

Here in this laboratory handbook author has tried to display as much programming codes of c programming as possible; but if students want they can perform other programming also after realising the basic principle of C programming because the basic structure of programming is same. But before that students must learn the theory properly related to C programming what is actually necessary for them.

[ANNEXTURE BOOK-4]

A SHORT HANDBOOK OF FUNDAMENTAL PROGRAMMING OF MATLAB FOR PRACTICE PURPOSE

INDEX

SL NO	NAME OF THE CHAPTER	PAGE NO
1	INTRODUCTION	132
2	GENERATION OF TRIGONOMETRIC WAVEFORM	132-133
3	GENERATION OF DIFFERENT SIGNALS	133-134
4	BASIC ARTITHMATIC AND ALGEBRA APPLICATIONS BY MATLAB	135-138
5	SOME BASIC TRIGONOMETRIC APPLICATION BY MATLAB	138-140
6	BASIC SALARY CALCULATION OF AN EMPLOYEE BY MATLAB	140
7	CONCLUSION	140

CHAPTER-1

INTRODUCTION

Mat-lab is a mathematical toolbox , that can solve all the mathematical problems just by using command; author has already done so many work on mat-lab; now in this last part of the book author has prescribed a genuine guidance to the students to know mat-lab from the grass-root. That means author wants that students must learn each and every command of mat-lab like what author has displayed in the previous C programming laboratory handbook. So, this is a simple hand book related to mat-lab for the students to learn the use of basic commands of mat-lab. The book can be useful for graduate level of engineering if students want to practise mat-lab as laboratory purpose. The author has added one of his research article at the end of the book so that graduate engineering students can understand the mat-lab related mathematical commands used in several programming purpose.

CHAPTER-2

GENERATION OF TRIGONOMETRIC WAVEFORM

2.1 PROGRAMMING CODES:

```
syms x t w
t=0:.1:5;
subplot(2,2,1)
w=100;
x=10*sin(w*t);
plot(x);
title('sine wave');
subplot(2,2,2)
w=100;
x=10*cos(w*t);
plot(x);
title('cosine wave');
subplot(2,2,3)
w=100;
x=10*tan(t);
```

```
plot(x);
title('tangent wave');
```


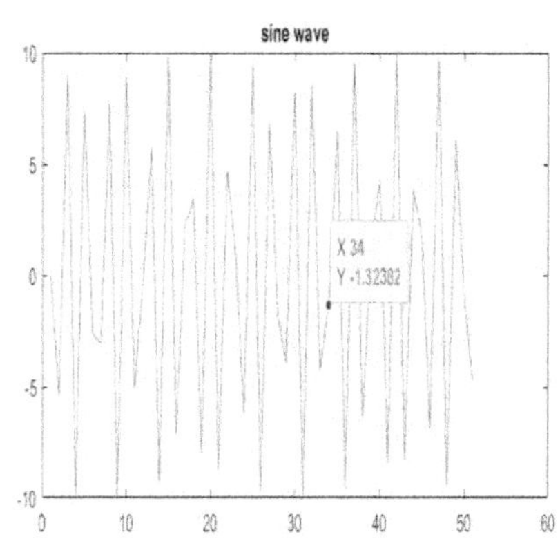

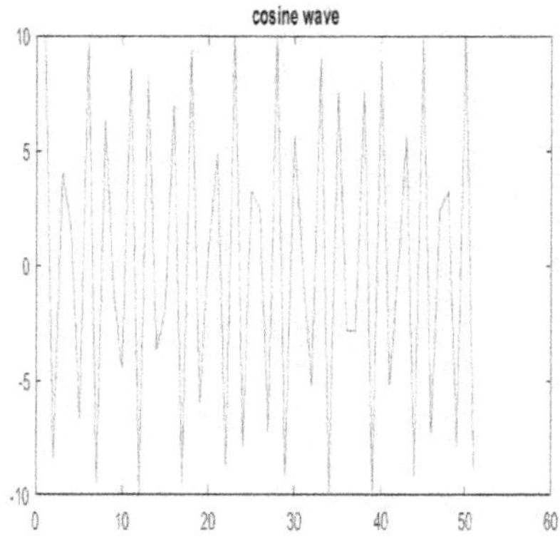

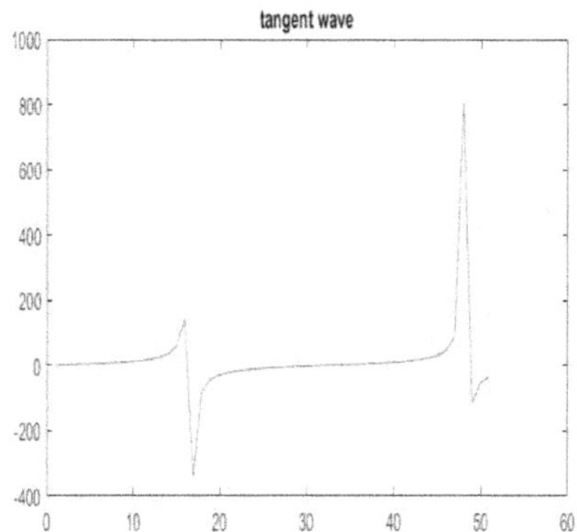

CHAPTER-3

GENERATION OF DIFFERENT SIGNALS

3.1 PROGRAMMING CODES:

```
syms x t
t=(-1:0.01:1)';
impulse=t==0;
x=impulse;
plot(t,x);
title('impulse wave');
```

```
subplot(2,2,2)
unitstep=t>=0;
x=unitstep;
plot(t,x);
title('unitstep');
subplot(2,2,3)
ramp=t.*unitstep;
x=ramp;
plot(t,x);
title('ramp signal');
subplot(2,2,4)
quad=t.^2.*unitstep;
x=quad;
plot(t,x);
title('hyparabolic signal');
```

3.2 OUTPUT WAVEFORM

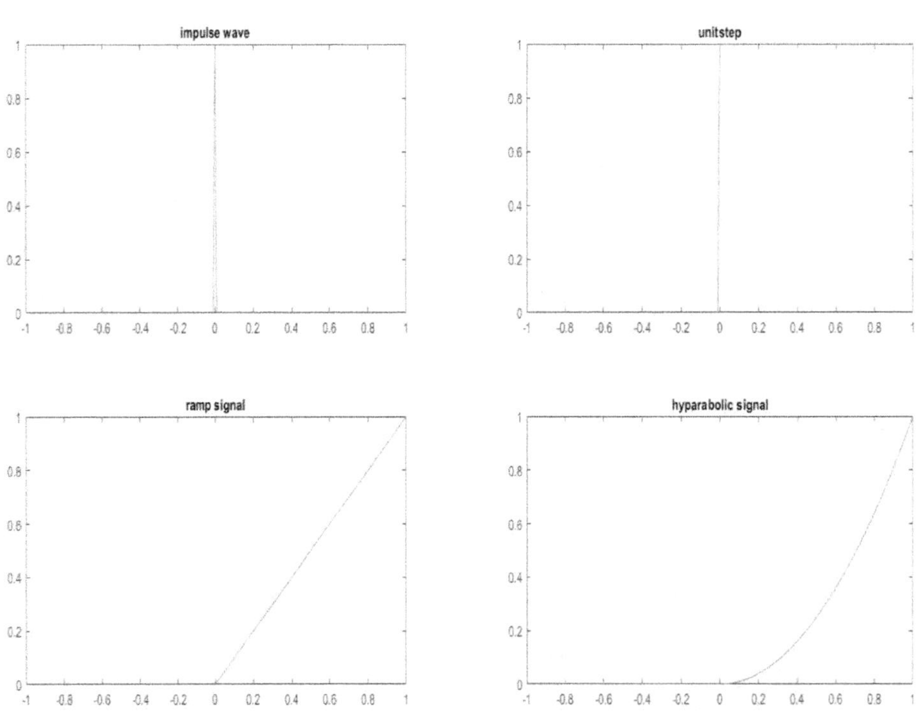

CHAPTER-4

BASIC ARTITHMATIC AND ALGEBRA APPLICATIONS BY MATLAB

4.1 PROGRAMMING CODES:

```
a. syms a b c
a=12;
b=9;
c=a+b;
c1=a-b;
c2=a*b;
c3=a/b;
c
c =

    21
c1
c1 =

    3
c2
c2 =

    108
c3
c3 =

    1.3333
a=12.5;
b=9.8;
c1=a+b;
c2=a-b;
c3=a*b;
c4=a/b;
c1
c1 =
```

```
   22.3000
c2
c2 =
   2.7000
c3
c3 =
  122.5000
c4
c4 =
   1.2755
```

b. syms a b

```
syms a b c
a=5;
b=4;
c=a^b;
c
c =
   625
```

c..

```
x=[6 8 10;12 15 17;13 18 20];
y=[2 4 6;8 10 12;11 13 17];
z=x+y;
z
z =
    8   12   16
   20   25   29
   24   31   37
z=x-y
z =
    4    4    4
    4    5    5
```

```
     2   5   3
z=x*y
z =
   186   234   302
   331   419   541
   390   492   634
eig(x)
ans =
  41.5423 + 0.0000i
  -0.2712 + 0.6753i
  -0.2712 - 0.6753i
det(x)
ans =

   22.0000
eig(y)
ans =
   29.9741
   -1.5059
    0.5317
inv(x)
ans =
  -0.2727    0.9091   -0.6364
  -0.8636   -0.4545    0.8182
   0.9545   -0.1818   -0.2727
inv(y)
ans =
  -0.5833   -0.4167    0.5000
   0.1667    1.3333   -1.0000
   0.2500   -0.7500    0.5000
```

```
det(y)
ans =
   -24
d. syms i1 i2 M L1 L2 x t k
L1=.28;
L2=.07;
k=.02;
M=k*sqrt(L1*L2);
M
M =
   0.0028
i1=10*cos(5*t);
i2=20*cos(10*t);
x=L1*diff(i1)-M*diff(i2);
y=L2*diff(i1)-M*diff(i2);
x
x =
(14*sin(10*t))/25 - 14*sin(5*t)
y
y =
(14*sin(10*t))/25 - (7*sin(5*t))/2
```

CHAPTER-5

SOME BASIC TRIGONOMETRIC APPLICATION BY MATLAB

```
a=60;
b=deg2rad(a);
b
b =
   1.0472
sin(b)
ans =
```

```
   0.8660
x=asin(0.8660)

x =

   1.0471

y=rad2deg(x)

y =

   59.9971==60

syms a b
a=30;
b=15;
x=deg2rad(a);
y=deg2rad(b);
x

x =

   0.5236

y

y =

   0.2618

sin(x)

ans =

   0.5000

sin(y)

ans =

   0.2588

sin(x+y)==sin(x)*cos(y)+cos(x)*sin(y);
sin(x+y)

ans =

   0.7071

cos(x+y)==cos(x)*cos(y)-sin(x)*sin(y);
cos(x+y)

ans =
```

0.7071

CHAPTER-6

BASIC SALARY CALCULATION OF AN EMPLOYEE BY MATLAB

```
syms basicsalary TA DA HRA MEDICAL TOTAL
basicsalary=15600;
TA=.1*basicsalary;
DA=.15*basicsalary;
HRA=.2*basicsalary;
MEDICAL=.18*basicsalary;
TOTAL=basicsalary+TA+DA+HRA+MEDICAL;
TOTAL
TOTAL =
    25428
```

CHAPTER-7

CONCLUSION

Here in this short handbook of mat-lab the aim of the author is to make the engineering graduate students aware how mathematical operations can be done primarily with the help of mat-lab; that's why author has skipped many critical point of views related to mat-lab and author has added one research article based on control system engineering related to mat-lab because author wants that in future students must use mat-lab for their research methodology based analysis; that research article is a total mathematical applications of mat-lab. So students can learn some new mathematical formulae's and related application from that research article. Very simple syntaxes are available in mat-lab help division so students can get some new syntaxes easily for mathematical applications from mat-lab help but they must know the necessary field where the applications are important. Author has used only small problems for the students just for practicing mat-lab as a beginner.

COMPARISON OF GAIN MARGIN AND PHASE MARGIN ALONG WITH SEVERAL OTHER PARAMETERIC COEFFICIENTS OF A SECOND ORDER SYSTEM UNDER DIFFERENT DAMPING CONDITIONS- A MATLAB SYNTAX BASED APPLICATION OF CONTROL SYSTEM ENGINEERING

[ABIR CHAKRABORTY 1 (RESEARCH SCIENTIST), DR.ABHIJIT BHOWMIK2 (ASSOCIATE PROFESSOR)

[VELLORE INSTITUTE OF TECHNOLOGY, VIT UNIVERSITY] (DEEMED UNIVERSITY), VELLORE, TAMILNADU , INDIA [PIN CODE-632014]

[**ABSTRACT** : This paper is an application of control system where we have used second order system in laplacian domain to find out the gain and phase margin. But before realising this we have calculated several parameters like Rise time, Peak time, natural and damping frequency under different damping conditions. Here we have used for types of damping factors; Underdamping, Critical damping, Over-damping and Oscillatory wave. For each cased we have used different transfer functions to generate gain phase margin and in whole paper we have displayed a comparison between above mentioned parameters how are they varying as per different damping conditions. For stability analysis we have used bode plot; all mat-lab syntaxes are available try to use it scientifically.]

INTRODUCTION:

 Before discussing about the main topic of the paper let's discuss about the basic of control system engineering technology. Transfer function is a key factor of control system programming. The main definition of '' Transfer function'' is something like that;

The TRANSFER FUNCTION is defined by

C(s)/R(s)=LAPLACE TRANSFORM OF OUTPUT FUNCTION/LAPLACE TRANSFORM OF INPUT FUNCTION

C(s)/R(s)=G(s)/1+G(s)H(s) Where G(S)= forward path gain in laplacian-domain , H(S)=feedbackpath gain in laplacian domain.

The transfer function has two important terminologies ; poles and zeroes,

POLES: Let us consider a transfer function

C(s)/R(s)=(S-Z1)*(S-Z2)*(S-Z3)*(S-Z4)/(S-P1)*(S-P2)*(S-P3)*(S-P4)

So pole means the value or the values for which the entire numerical value of the transfer function of a control system unit will tend to infinity.

ZEROES: Let us consider a transfer function

C(s)/R(s)=(S-Z1)*(S-Z2)*(S-Z3)*(S-Z4)/(S-P1)*(S-P2)*(S-P3)*(S-P4)

Therefore, zero means the value or the values for which the entire numerical value of the entire transfer function of a control-system unit will tend to zero.

Now we should know the terminologies applied in this paper regarding a second order system;

One by one we are discussing these terminologies;

RISE TIME: The rise time is the time needed for the response to reach from 10% to 90% or 0% to 100% of the desired value of the output at the very instant;

PEAK TIME: It is the instant of occurring the maximum overshoot

wn is the natural frequency of oscillation

wd is called damping frequency of oscillation wd=wnsqrt(1-geta^2)

geta= So called damping constant determining the nature of damping

geta>1 OVER-DAMPED OSCILLATION

geta<1 UNDERDAMPED OSCILLATION

geta=1 CRITICALLY DAMPED

Based on those damping factor we have designed the step plot analysis;

Lets talk about the stability analysis of the entire second order system under different damping conditions for which we have used BODE PLOT analysis. Now the question is that there are NYQUIST PLOT or NICHOLE'S CHART ANALYSIS but still we have used BODE PLOT because mat-lab syntaxes are easy to obtain and use in this case as well as we are determining and comparing the GAIN MARGIN and PHASE MARGIN anaslysis for which we need to know the technology of BODE PLOT. BODE PLOT is a method of ABSOLUTE STABILITY. Which judges whether the system is absolutely stable or unstable. So you need to know the necessity of 'GAIN MARGIN' and 'PHASE MARGIN'.

GAIN MARGIN: The gain margin refers to the amount of gain which can be increased or decreased without making the system unstable. It is expressed in DB.

PHASE MARGIN: Phase margin. Phase margin is defined as the amount of change in open-loop phase needed to make a closed-loop system unstable. The phase margin is the difference in phase between $-180°$ and the phase at the gain cross-over frequency that gives a gain of 0 dB.

So for some extra work we have calculated the phase and gain cross over frequency co related to gain or phase margin respectively.

[NOTE: Before realising the process of programming the reviewer must note that for all four different damping conditions we have fixed the damping constants in programming for the corresponding transfer functions by using mat-lab syntaxes in each case for each table so that you can understand the transfer functions values based on the nature of damping.

PROCESS OF PROGRAMMING:

STEP 1: Define the necessary terminologies of a second order system in mat-lab

STEP 2: Fixed the values of natural frequency of oscillation (wn) and damping factor

STEP 3: Arrange the transfer function of Over-damped, Under damped, Critically damped and An pure Oscillatory system through different damping factors as per definitions.

STEP 4: Use subplot technology to find out the STEP analysis of types of damping system of second order.

STEP 5: Find out the numerical values terminologies that you have mentioned as mat-lab syntaxes to prepare a table;

STEP 6: Same way find out Gain and Phase margin with gain and phase crossover frequency to prepare another table.

STEP 7: Find out the pole zero plot for all the damping conditions in a single window by using ''Subplot'' technology and prepare a table which contains the values of poles under different damping constants with locations in complex 'S' plane.

3. MATLAB CODES OF PROGRAMMING:

[NOTE: All throughout the programming we have used different damping constants for four different conditions of damping but same natural frequency of oscillation; if you want to change values of damping constants in each case you can do it but four different damping conditions must be maintained depending on damping constant geta; different mat-lab syntaxes can be used to find out the step plots.]

3.1 PROGRAMMING CODE OF TIME RESPONSE OF SECOND ORDER CONTROL SYSTEM

```
subplot(2,2,1)
syms wn1 s wd1 tp1 tr1 phi1 sys1 geta1
wn1=10;
geta1=.5;
wd1=wn1*sqrt(1-geta1^2);
tp1=pi/wd1;
sys1 = tf(10,[1 2*.5*10 10^2]);
phi1=atan(sqrt(1-geta1^2)/geta1);
tr1=(pi-phi1)/wd1;
step(sys1);
title('underdamped response');
subplot(2,2,2)
syms wn2 s wd2 tp2 tr2 phi2 sys2 geta2
geta2=0;
wn2=10;
wd2=wn2*sqrt(1-geta2^2);
tp2=pi/wd2;
sys2 = tf(10,[1 2*0*10 10^2]);
phi2=atan(sqrt(1-geta2^2)/geta2);
 tr2=(pi-phi2)/wd2;
step(sys2);
title('oscillatory wave');
subplot(2,2,3)
syms wn3 s wd3 tp3 tr3 phi3 sys3 geta3
wn3=10;
geta3=1;
wd3=wn3*sqrt(1-geta3^2);
tp3=pi/wd3;
```

```
sys3 = tf(10,[1 2*1*10 10^2]);

phi3=atan(sqrt(1-geta3^2)/geta3);

tr3=(pi-phi3)/wd3;

step(sys3);

title('critical response');

subplot(2,2,4)

syms wn4 s wd4 tp4 tr4 phi4 sys4 geta4

wn4=10;

geta4=1.5;

wd4=wn4*sqrt(1-geta4^2);

tp4=pi/wd4;

sys4 = tf(10,[1 2*1.5*10 10^2]);

phi4=atan(sqrt(1-geta4^2)/geta4);

tr4=(pi-phi4)/wd4;

step(sys4);

title('ovardamped response');
```

3.2 PROGRAMMING CODE OF BODE PLOT OF SECOND ORDER CONTROL SYSTEM WITH DIFFERENT DAMPING

```
subplot(2,2,1)

syms wn1 s wd1 tp1 tr1 phi1 sys1 geta1

wn1=10;

geta1=.5;

wd1=wn1*sqrt(1-geta1^2);

sys1 = tf(10,[1 2*.5*10 10^2]);

bode(sys1);

title('bode plot of underdamped response');

subplot(2,2,2)

syms wn2 s wd2 tp2 tr2 phi2 sys2 geta2

geta2=0;

wn2=10;

wd2=wn2*sqrt(1-geta2^2);

sys2 = tf(10,[1 2*0*10 10^2]);

bode(sys2);

title('bode plot of oscillatory wave');

subplot(2,2,3)

syms wn3 s wd3 tp3 tr3 phi3 sys3 geta3
```

```matlab
wn3=10;
geta3=1;
wd3=wn3*sqrt(1-geta3^2);
sys3 = tf(10,[1 2*1*10 10^2]);
bode(sys3);
title('bode plot of critical response');
subplot(2,2,4)
syms wn4 s wd4 tp4 tr4 phi4 sys4 geta4
wn4=10;
geta4=1.5;
wd4=wn4*sqrt(1-geta4^2);
sys4 = tf(10,[1 2*1.5*10 10^2]);
bode(sys4);
title('bode plot of ovardamped response');
```

3.3 PROGRAMMING CODE OF POLE ZERO PLOT OF SECOND ORDER CONTROL SYSTEM WITH DIFFERENT DAMPING

```matlab
subplot(2,2,1)
syms wn1 s sys1 geta1
wn1=10;
geta1=.5;
sys1 = tf(10,[1 2*.5*10 10^2]);
pzmap(sys1);
title('pole zero plot of underdamped response');
subplot(2,2,2)
syms wn2 s sys2 geta2
wn2=10;
geta2=0;
sys2 = tf(10,[1 2*0*10 10^2]);
pzmap(sys2);
title('pole zero plot of oscillatory response');
subplot(2,2,3)
syms wn3 s sys3 geta3
wn3=10;
geta3=1;
sys3 = tf(10,[1 2*1*10 10^2]);
```

```
pzmap(sys3);

title('pole zero plot of critically damped response');

subplot(2,2,4)

syms wn4 s sys4 geta4

wn4=10;

geta4=1.5;

sys4 = tf(10,[1 2*1.5*10 10^2]);

pzmap(sys4);

title('pole zero plot of over-damped response');
```

3.4 PROGRAMMING CODE OF GAIN AND PHASE MARGIN

```
syms wn1 s sys1 geta1

wn1=10;

geta1=.5;

sys1 = tf(10,[1 2*.5*10 10^2]);

[Gm,Pm,Wcg,Wcp] = margin(sys1)
```

4. STEP PLOT, BODE-PLOT AND POLE-ZERO PLOT OF SECOND ORDER SYSTEM WITH DIFFERENT DAMPING FACTORS

4.1STEP PLOT OUTCOMES

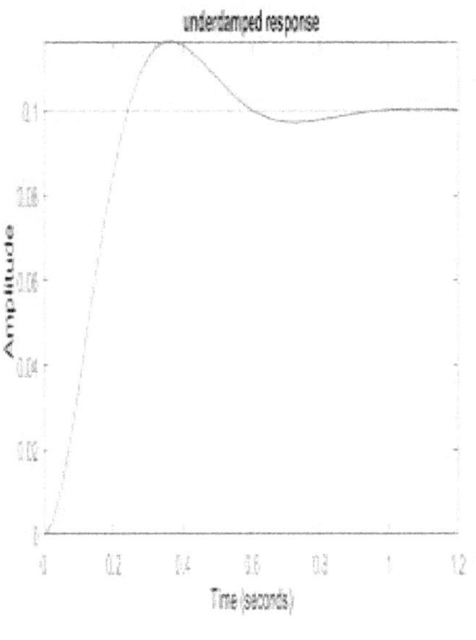
underdamped response

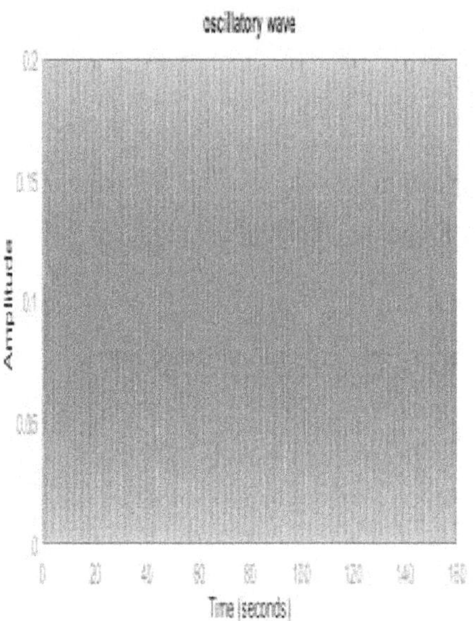
oscillatory wave

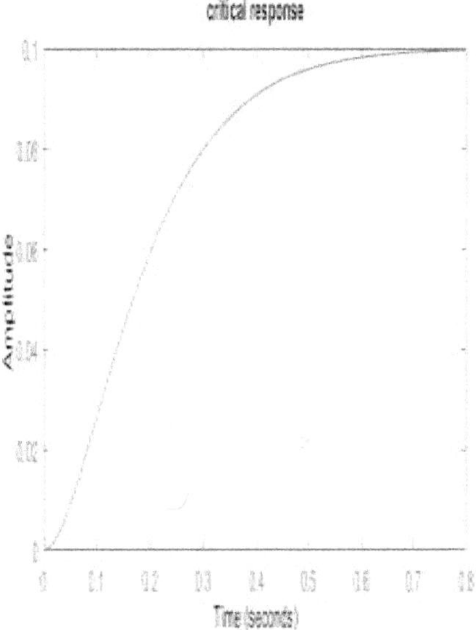
critical response

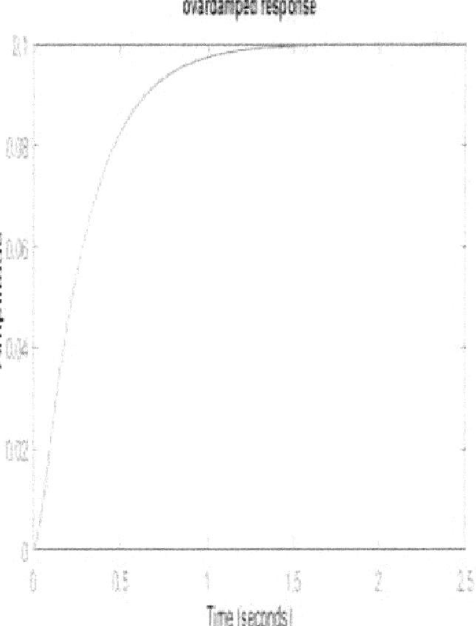
ovardamped response

BODE PLOT OUTCOMES

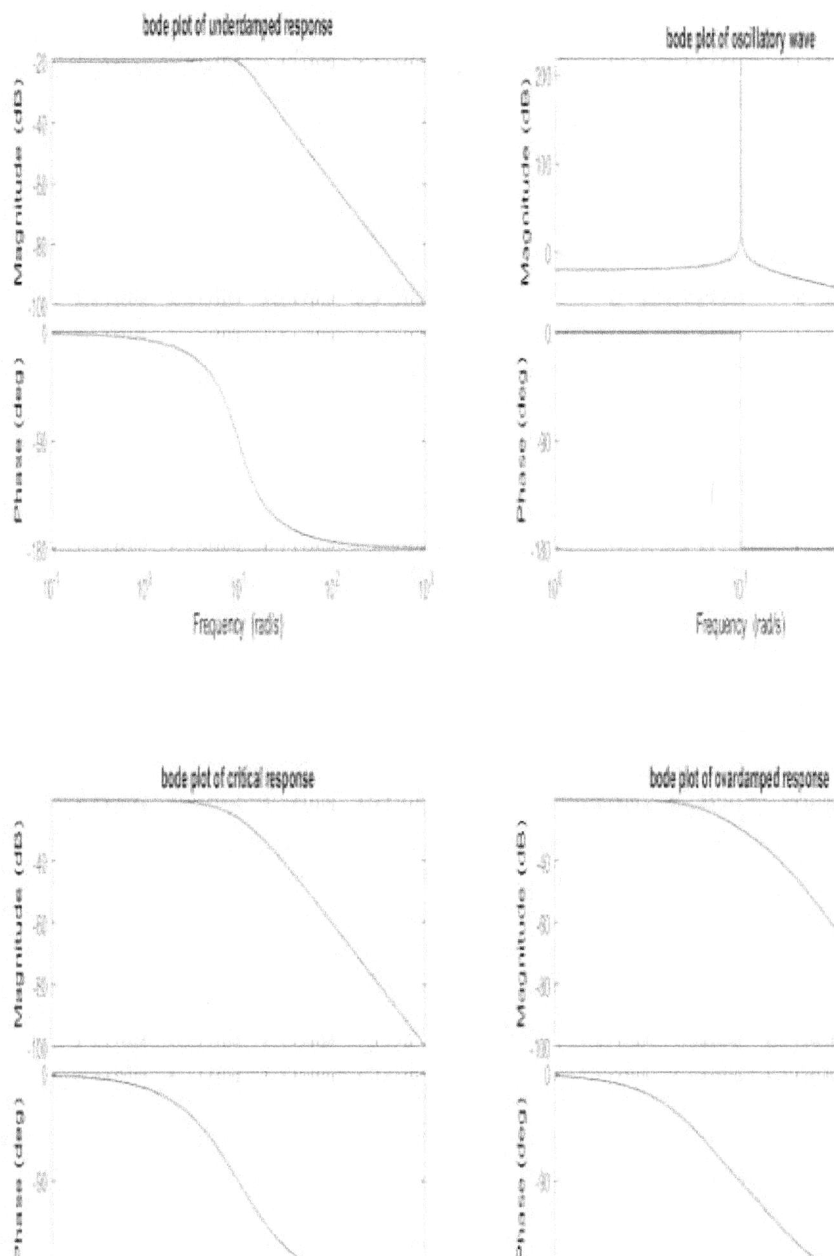

POLE ZERO PLOT

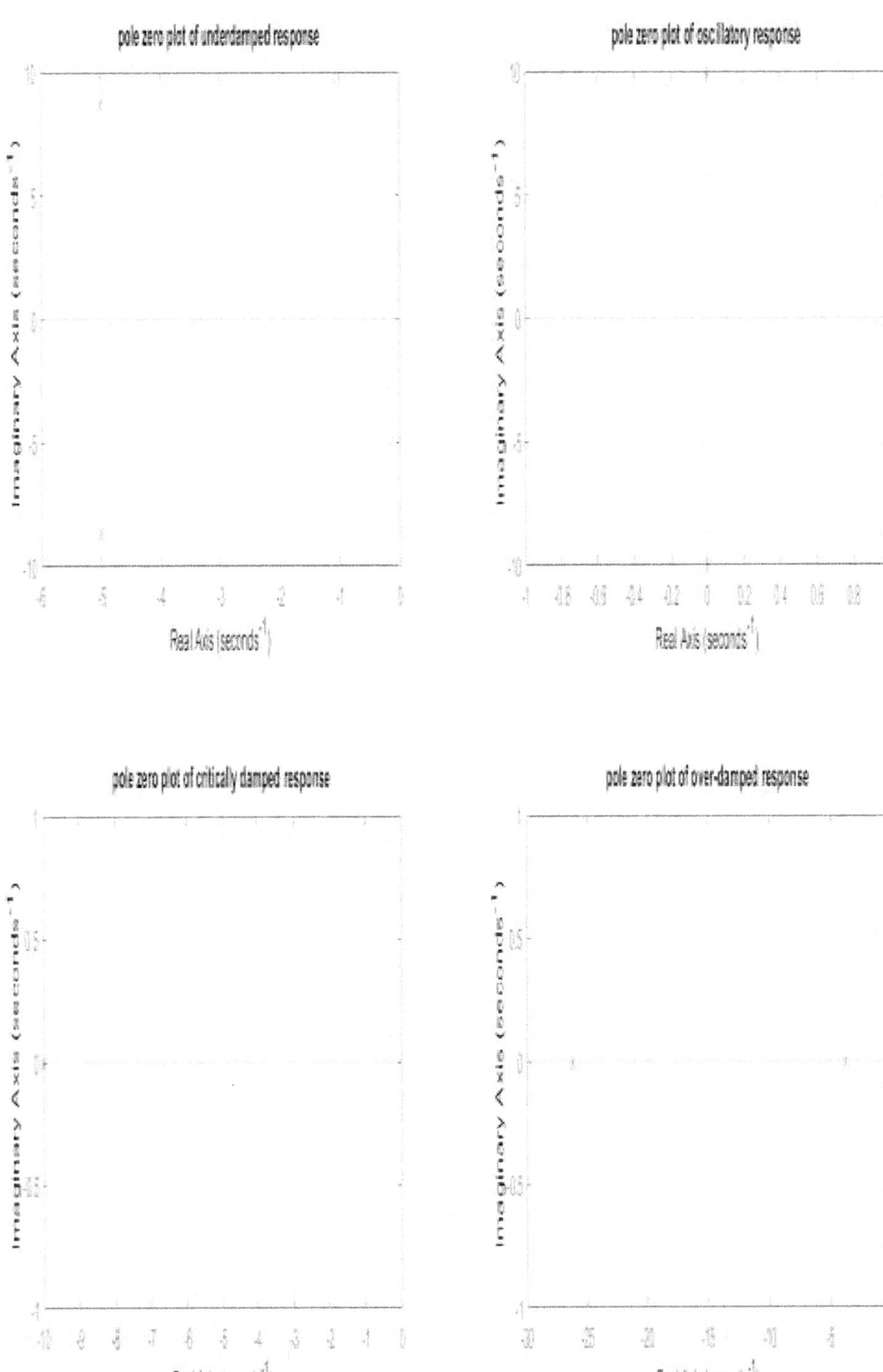

TABULAR FORM OF MATLAB REALTED CALCULATIONS

[NOTE: If you change the values of damping constants in each case then the values of transfer functions as well as other parameters will be changed in each case. But be cautious about the four different nature of damping conditions used in this programming.]

5.1 TABLE NO.1 CALCULATIONS OF SECOND ORDER SYSTEM RELATED PARAMETERS

Geta= Damping factor

tr = Rise time

tp = Peak time

wn= Natural frequency of oscillation

wd=Damping frequency of oscillation

phi= Tangential angle of damping

NATURE OF DAMPING	TRANSFER FUNCTION	geta	tr	tp	wn	wd	phi
Under damped	$\dfrac{10}{s^2 + 10\,s + 100}$	0.5000	0.2418	0.3628	10	8.6603	1.0472
Oscillatory	$\dfrac{10}{s^2 + 100}$	0	0.1571	0.3142	10	10	1.5708
Critically damped	$\dfrac{10}{s^2 + 20\,s + 100}$	1	Infinity	Infinity	10	0	0
Over damped	$\dfrac{10}{s^2 + 30\,s + 100}$	1.5	-0.0861 - 0.2810i	0.0000 - 0.2810i	10	0.0000 +11.1803i	0.0000 + 0.9624i

5.2 TABLE NO.2 TABLE OF CALCULATIONS OF GAIN AND PHASE MARGIN USIING MATLAB CODES

NATURE OF DAMPING	TRANSFER FUNCTION	Gain margin	Phase margin	Gain crossover frequency	Phase crossover frequency
Under damped	$\dfrac{10}{s^2 + 10\,s + 100}$	Infinity	Infinity	Infinity	NaN
Oscillatory	$\dfrac{10}{s^2 + 100}$	Infinity	0	Infinity	10.4882
Critically damped	$\dfrac{10}{s^2 + 20\,s + 100}$	Infinity	Infinity	Infinity	NaN
Over damped	$\dfrac{10}{s^2 + 30\,s + 100}$	Infinity	Infinity	Infinity	NAN

	s^2 + 30 s + 100				

5.3 TABLE NO.3 DETERMINE THE VALUES AND LOCATION OF POLES IN 'S' PLANE OR IN COMPLEX PLANE FOR ALL TYPES OF DAMPING CONSTANTS

NATURE OF DAMPING	TRANSFER FUNCTION	POLE	Location of poles
Under damped	10 ---------------- s^2 + 10 s + 100	-5.0000 + 8.6603i -5.0000 - 8.6603i	Left half of 'S' plane S=sigma +j*w
Oscillatory	10 --------- s^2 + 100	0.0000 +10.0000i 0.0000 -10.0000i	On imaginary axis of 'S ' plane
Critically damped	10 ---------------- s^2 + 20 s + 100	-10, -10	Left half of 'S' plane on X-axis
Over damped	10 ---------------- s^2 + 30 s + 100	-26.1803, -3.8197	Left half of 'S' plane on X-axis

DISCUSSIONS OF RESULTS:

Look at the table 1 very carefully Rise time and Peak time both are maximum in a critically damped system but if you look at table 2 very carefully you can see that gain and phase margin all are infinity in most of the cases. Now depending on the value of geta or damping factor the transfer function changes. Mat-lab syntaxes are available you may find out the settling time for each damping factors.

CONCLUSIONS:

Here we have used BODE PLOT analysis to define the stability of the transfer function. But if you want you can use NYQUIST PLOT or NICHOLE'S PLOT analysis. In NYQUIST PLOT there is a point called ' Critical Point' which is -1+j0 ; you will have to observe that how many times the plot encircles the critical point. Exactly the same number of poles lie in the right half of s-plane and the entire system becomes unstable otherwise if not encircles the critical point then the system is stable. Here in this paper we have not taken any help from other journals to write the codes. We have followed a book on LINEAR CONTROL SYSTEM-composed by author B.S.MANKE to define the second order system related terminologies. So you are requested to write your codes by your own techniques. But you cannot detect gain and phase margin from NYQUIST PLOT or NICHOLE'S PLOT.

FUTURE SCOPE OF WORK:

We have done step response analysis of each transfer function; try to implement this concept by using 'impulse response ' and see the changes in the outcomes; if you want you can change the values of natural frequency(wn) or damping factor(geta) but the conditions of all types of damping must remain same ; therefore choose the damping constants very carefully.

REFERENCES:

a.'LINEAR CONTROL SYSTEM'-with mat-lab application- Prof. B.S.Manke